PANAMA
in Pictures

Tom Streissguth

Lerner Publications Company

Contents

Website address: www.lernerbooks.co

Lerner Publications Company
A division of Lerner Publishing Group
241 First Avenue North
Minneapolis, MN 55401 U.S.A.

web enhanced @ www.vgsbooks.com

CULTURAL LIFE 46

▶ Music. Language, Literature, and Communications. Arts and Crafts. Religion. Festivals and Holidays. Sports and Recreation. Foods of Panama.

THE ECONOMY 58

▶ Services. Manufacturing. Farming. Mining and Energy. Foreign Trade. Transportation. The Future.

FOR MORE INFORMATION

Library of Congress Cataloging-in-Publication Data

Streissguth, Thomas, 1958-
    Panama in pictures / by Thomas Streissguth.
        p.   cm. — (Visual geography series)
    Includes bibliographical references and index.
    ISBN: 0-8225-2395-7 (lib. bdg. : alk. paper)
    1. Panama—Juvenile literature. I. Title. II. Series: Visual geography series (Minneapolis, Minn.)
F1563.2.S77 2005
972.87'054'0222—dc22   2004017910

Manufactured in the United States of America
1 2 3 4 5 6 - BP - 10 09 08 07 06 05

INTRODUCTION

Panama is a nation in Central America. It is located on the Isthmus of Panama between North and South America. The isthmus (a narrow strip of land connecting two larger land areas) also sits between the Caribbean Sea (part of the Atlantic Ocean) and the Pacific Ocean. This location between continents and oceans has made Panama a cross-roads of shipping and international trade. Panama has benefited greatly from the Panama Canal, a human-made waterway that links the two oceans. Designed by engineers from France and the United States and built primarily by Panamanian and Caribbean laborers, the canal has made Panama's trade and transportation businesses possible. But the canal also has caused conflict between Panama and the United States, as well as political and social turmoil within Panama.

The first Panamanians were Native Americans, who migrated (traveled) to the Isthmus of Panama at least ten thousand years ago. These people lived in villages in mountain valleys and along sea-coasts. Their leaders, known as caciques, ruled one or several villages

each. No single cacique ever controlled a large area of Panama, however. Because of its location, ancient Panama was an important center of trade between native peoples from Central and South America.

Spanish explorers arrived in the Americas in the sixteenth century. Panama, along with other parts of North, Central, and South America, became a colony of Spain (a territory under Spanish control). Spanish settlers mined gold and silver in the Americas and shipped it back to Spain. Many ships filled with riches departed from Panama's ports on the Caribbean Sea. Pirates, or outlaw sailors, frequently attacked these ships and Panama's ports in search of treasure.

When Colombia, to the south of Panama, gained its independence from Spain in 1819, Panama became a province of Colombia. With the help of the U.S. government, Panama gained its own independence in 1903. Eleven years later, the United States completed the Panama Canal. Although Panamanians governed their own nation, the Canal Zone (the stretch of land containing the canal) was under U.S. control.

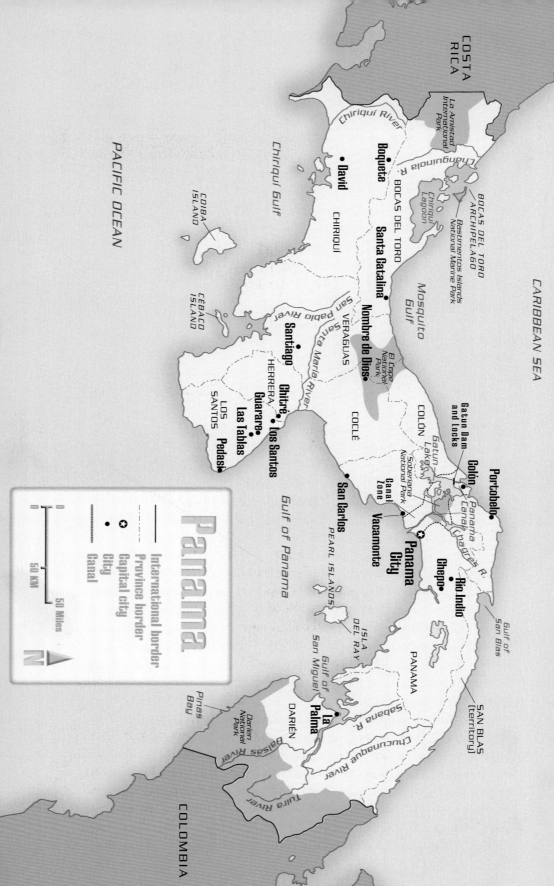

The Panama Canal brought trade and business to Panama, which became the wealthiest nation in Central America. Banking, foreign trade, transportation, and tourism prospered in the major cities of Colón and Panama City. Although some people in the cities grew rich, most people in the countryside remained isolated and poor. The government did not treat all people equally. For instance, Native Americans did not enjoy the same rights as people descended from Spanish settlers. Black Panamanians (descendants of workers who had come to build the canal and the Panama Railroad) were also denied civil rights. A complex mix of cultures, combined with political instability and harsh rulers, made Panama a troubled land. More trouble arrived in 1989, when the United States invaded Panama to overthrow Manuel Noriega, a military dictator accused of allowing drug traffickers to operate in Panama.

Despite these hardships, Panama created its own cultural identity in the twentieth century. Panamanian writers described the country's turbulent society and its efforts to break free of foreign influences and establish its own identity. Panamanian artists drew on native arts and crafts as inspiration for their own works, while musicians adopted Caribbean dance styles, such as calypso and salsa.

In 1999, after many years of debate, negotiations, and violence, the United States turned the Panama Canal over to Panama. With the canal finally under their own control, Panamanians will profit even more from its operation. But Panama remains vulnerable to shifts in the world economy. When foreign trade falters, Panama suffers. For instance, after the terrorist attacks on the United States in September 2001, trade and tourism decreased in Panama, causing a sharp rise in unemployment. In addition, as cargo ships get increasingly larger, the viability of the canal is threatened.

Despite frustration with their political leaders and uncertainty over their economic future, Panamanians feel proud of their nation and its accomplishments. Panama's control over the Panama Canal, achieved on the last day of the twentieth century, gave the nation a reason to celebrate. The nation's standing as a center of international trade and service industries also offers opportunities for a prosperous future.

THE LAND

The Republic of Panama, located at the southeastern end of Central America, covers an area of 29,157 square miles (75,517 square kilometers). It is slightly smaller than the state of South Carolina. The country stretches more than 400 miles (644 km) from west to east. From north to south, the country measures 130 miles (209 km) at its widest. Panama has two land boundaries, a 205-mile (330-km) border on the west with Costa Rica and a 140-mile (225-km) frontier on the east with Colombia. The Caribbean Sea forms Panama's northern border, with 470 miles (760 km) of coastline. Panama's southern border is the Pacific Ocean, with a rugged coastline about 760 miles (1,225 km) long.

Geographical Regions

Panama has three major geographical regions: the Atlantic Lowlands in the north, the Pacific Lowlands in the south, and the Central Highlands in the interior. The Atlantic and Pacific lowlands cover

level terrain below 3,000 feet (914 meters) in elevation. The Central Highlands feature high plains, deep river valleys, and mountains towering more than 5,000 feet (1,524 m) in elevation.

The Atlantic Lowlands along the Caribbean coast contain forests, farmland, and the city of Colón, which lies at the Atlantic entrance to the Panama Canal. Several archipelagoes (groups of islands), including the Bocas del Toro Archipelago in the west and the San Blas Islands in the east, line the coast. The Chiriquí Lagoon and the Mosquito Gulf form large bays on the Caribbean coast.

The Pacific Lowlands, including the Chiriquí Gulf in the west and the Gulf of Panama in the east, face the Pacific Ocean. In between the two gulfs lies the flat and humid Azuero Peninsula. Like the Atlantic Lowlands, the Pacific Lowlands hold forests and farmland. Panama City, the nation's capital, sits on the Pacific coast at the southern end of the Panama Canal. Coiba Island and Cébaco Island lie just west of the Azuero Peninsula, while the Gulf of Panama contains Contadora Island, Taboga Island, the Pearl Islands, and Isla del Rey.

The Central Highlands cover Panama's interior. This is an area of high mountains and scattered small towns. Farms are located in valleys between the mountains. The tallest peaks of the interior are found in the Tabasará Mountains in the western half of the country. This range straddles the border with Costa Rica and gradually lessens in height as it runs east toward the Panama Canal. Panama's highest point, the Barú Volcano, is located in this range. It measures 11,401 feet (3,475 m) above sea level. The San Blas Mountains rise along Panama's northeastern coast, while the Darién Mountains straddle Panama's border with Colombia. The Majé Mountains run along the southeastern coast. A wilderness region called the Darién Gap, filled with thick forests and rushing rivers, covers the far eastern interior. Much of Darién has not been thoroughly explored or mapped.

THE DARIÉN GAP

The Darién Gap region is a true wilderness, where many areas of dense rain forest *(right)* remain unmapped and unexplored. The region is named for the break, or gap, in the Pan American Highway. This road runs from Mexico to the southern tip of South America, except for an uncompleted stretch in Darién. The Darién Gap not only prevents road travel along the highway but also stops the transmission of deadly diseases, such as hoof-and-mouth disease, from one continent to the next.

Water rushes through a **stream** in a mountain valley of western Panama.

Rivers and Waterways

Panama's most famous geographical feature is the Panama Canal, a 40-mile (65-km) waterway linking the Pacific and Atlantic oceans. The human-made canal, first opened in 1914, is 300 feet (91 m) wide and 41 feet (13 m) deep—large enough to accommodate big oceangoing ships. The canal runs between the cities of Colón and Panama City. On its northern end, the canal route passes through Gatun Lake, a large artificial lake created by the damming of the Chagres River during construction of the canal.

Panama holds many natural waterways, including several hundred rivers that originate in the Central Highlands and crisscross the country. Fed by heavy rains and springs, these shallow and short waterways drain Panama's mountain valleys. In the west, the Changuinola River flows due north into the Chiriquí Lagoon. The San Pablo River and the Santa María River run along the northern limits of the Azuero Peninsula and empty into the Pacific Ocean. In the east, the principal rivers are the Chucunaque, Balsas, Tuira, and Sabana. Hundreds of streams, many of them not yet named, run through the Darién Gap. At the Pacific port of La Palma, the Tuira and Sabana rivers empty into the Gulf of San Miguel, part of the Gulf of Panama.

Climate

Panama has a year-round warm climate, with two main seasons. The dry season runs from December to May, and the rainy season lasts for the rest of the year. Heavy thunderstorms and rain showers occur frequently, even during the dry season. The rains are heaviest on the Caribbean coast, which records 150 inches (381 centimeters) of rainfall every year, one of the highest rates in the world. Because Panama receives so much rain, it is also very humid, especially in lowlands and coastal areas.

In the Pacific and Atlantic lowlands, the average temperature is about 80°F (27°C) year-round. The Central Highlands are cooler. Temperatures there range from 50°F (10°C) to 70°F (21°C), depending on the time of year. The coolest time of year is the dry season, when frost can appear in the mountains.

Flora and Fauna

Panama has an abundance of plants and animals. Many varieties of monkeys live in the nation's forests, as do jaguars, ocelots, and other cats. One of the country's most unusual animals is the capybara, a giant rodent that can grow to 4 feet (1.2 m) in length. Another interesting Panamanian animal is the sloth. Sloths are slow-moving animals that spend most of their lives hanging upside down from tree branches. They can even sleep hanging upside down.

Panama is also home to 954 native bird species—more than the number of bird species in all of North America. One of the largest

The **capybara** is the world's largest rodent.

Panama's national bird, the **harpy eagle**, is an endangered species. Find out more about Panama's wildlife by checking out the links at www.vgsbooks.com.

birds is the harpy eagle (Panama's national bird), which lives by preying on smaller birds and mammals. Five species of macaws (a kind of parrot), as well as toucans, umbrella birds, quetzals, and parakeets thrive in forests. Freshwater fish include the killifish and the armored catfish. Black marlins, sharks, dolphins, and barracudas swim in coastal waters and along offshore coral reefs.

Dense thickets of tropical mangrove trees line the coasts of Panama. About one-third of the nation is covered by rain forests. These forests are home to a variety of plants, including more than 1,200 types of orchids—beautiful flowering plants that grow on the trunks and branches of trees. Panama also hosts about 700 species of ferns and 1,500 different trees, including balsa, wild cashew, rubber, oak, and palm trees. Fruit trees include banana, coconut, guava, and papaya.

Quetzals are among the most colorful birds in Panama. They have glittering emerald green feathers on their heads, backs, and chests, with brilliant red feathers on their underparts. Their heads are topped by crests of golden green feathers. Male quetzals have long trains of tail feathers.

Natural Resources

Panama's natural resources include deposits of copper, gold, and other minerals, as well as coal. Panama extracts (digs up) and sells some of these resources. But some mineral deposits are located in areas where native peoples live. In these regions, people have passed laws against mining. Because of these laws, Panama has not mined all its mineral resources.

Panama's rain forests hold valuable tropical trees such as mahogany trees. Loggers cut the trees, which are then sold for construction and furniture making. Panama's coastal regions have rich beds of lobsters, shrimp, and other ocean shellfish, which are caught in traps or nets and sold for food. Only about 7 percent of Panama is arable, or suitable for farming. But Panama still profits from the sale of its farm crops, including bananas, coconuts, cacao beans, coffee beans, corn, and tobacco. Farmers also raise livestock, such as cattle, pigs, and chickens.

The fast-moving streams and rivers of Panama provide a valuable energy resource. The flowing water powers hydroelectric generators, which create electricity.

Environmental Issues

Like most nations, Panama suffers from environmental problems. For instance, large-scale logging has brought about deforestation—the destruction of large areas of forest. When trees and roots are

Panama's **rain forests** are home to about 10,000 different kinds of plants and about 1,000 species of birds.

cleared from the land, soil washes down hillsides. Rivers fill with mud, killing the plants and animals that live in the water.

In Panama, large areas around the Panama Canal have been cleared of trees. Mud has washed into the Panama Canal and settled on the bottom, making it more difficult for large ships to pass through. Mud also sometimes clogs the canal's locks, devices for raising and lowering boats as they pass through the canal.

Farming also causes environmental problems for Panama. For instance, fertilizers (chemicals that improve plant growth) and pesticides (chemicals that kill insects) run off from farmers' fields into Panamanian rivers. These chemicals sometimes poison the plants and animals that live in the rivers. They can also harm plants and animals that live along the seacoast.

The growth of cities, farms, and mines has also hurt Panama's rain forests. People have cut down forests to build houses, stores, roads, and other structures. When the forests are cut down, there are fewer places for forest plants and animals to live. Because of deforestation, howler monkeys and spider monkeys are endangered species (in danger of dying out) in Panama. Several species of birds and amphibians have become extinct, or died out altogether.

To protect its natural wealth, Panama has set aside fifteen national parks as well as ten wildlife sanctuaries and twelve nature reserves. Altogether, the government has protected about 29 percent of the country's land from development. The largest protected areas include La Amistad International Park, shared with Costa Rica in the west, and the Darién National Park, located along the Colombian border.

Cities

Panama has a population of more than 3 million people. Roughly 62 percent of them live in cities. The largest urban area is Panama City, the nation's capital. Other large cities include Colón, David, Santiago, and Chitré.

PANAMA CITY Panama's capital and largest city, Panama City (population 389,172) sits at the southern end of the Panama Canal. The city was founded in August 1519 by Pedro Arias de Ávila, a Spanish knight

In 1519 Spanish colonists founded a town and port along the Pacific coast of Central America. Local Indians nicknamed the settlement Panama, which meant "plenty of fish." The name soon came to apply to the whole country.

Panama City the capital of Panama, is a modern, thriving commercial center stretching 5 miles (8 km) along the Pacific coast.

and naval commander. During the 1500s and 1600s, the English pirates Francis Drake and Henry Morgan attacked the city frequently in search of gold and other loot. During one of Henry Morgan's assaults, in 1671, his forces set a fire that completely destroyed the city. Two years later, a Spanish governor founded a new Panama City 2 miles (3.2 km) to the west.

Panama City soon flourished. The city was a center of trade between Spain's South American colonies and the mother country of Spain. But as new cities grew in South America in the eighteenth century, Panama's importance declined. The city grew poorer, and many of its residents returned to Spain.

In the mid-nineteenth century, gold was discovered in California in the United States. Seeking fast transportation from the eastern United States to California, gold seekers took ships to Panama, crossed the isthmus on foot or mule, then boarded boats for the final leg of their journey to California. The gold rush traffic led to the building of the Panama Railroad across the isthmus. The railroad, in turn, helped revive Panama City's economy.

In the 1880s, the French made the first attempt to build a canal across Panama. This project also brought people and business to Panama City. After the French canal company failed, the canal was completed by the United States.

For centuries, explorers and traders in the Western Hemisphere wanted an easy way to travel between the Atlantic and Pacific oceans. At first, the only route was a dangerous sea voyage around Cape Horn at the southern tip of South America. This trip could take sailing ships several weeks or even months, depending on the weather.

The Panama Canal, completed in the early twentieth century, gave ships an easy route between oceans, saving time and money. A modern oceangoing ship can travel through the canal in about eight hours.

Panama City experienced rapid growth as well as frequent political turmoil during the twentieth century. During the mid-1900s, many city residents protested against U.S. control of the Panama Canal. In 1989 the United States invaded the city and captured President Manuel Noriega, who was accused of allowing drug traffickers (large-scale drug dealers) to operate in his country. The invasion did heavy damage to the city.

In modern times, Panama City is a mixture of old and new. The San Felipe neighborhood, on the south-western side of the city, holds the remains of the original Panama City. It also has the Presidential Palace, the popular Bolívar Plaza, the seventeenth-century Metropolitan Church, and a bustling banking district. A seafront neighborhood named Punta Paitilla has glittering shops and high-rise apartment buildings. In the northeastern corner of the city lie the Miraflores Locks, which allow ships to pass from the Panama Canal to sea level.

COLÓN With a population of 138,000, Colón is Panama's second largest city. It is located at the northern end of the Panama Canal. In 1850, American builders founded the city as a home for workers building the Panama Railroad and as a port for the delivery of construction supplies. The town was first named Aspinwall, in honor of one of the railroad's builders. In 1890 the name was changed to Colón (the Spanish version of Columbus), in honor of explorer Christopher Columbus.

The railroad and then the Panama Canal linking Colón to Panama City helped the city grow. In 1953 Panama established a free trade zone in Colón. Within this zone, companies can import and export goods free of taxes and other fees. The zone has brought new manufacturing and warehousing businesses to the city. Near Colón are the Gatun Locks, which raise and lower ships between the Panama Canal and the Atlantic Ocean, and Gatun Dam, both built during the canal's construction.

For links to websites where you can find out more about the cities of Panama—including Panama City, Colón, David, Santiago, and Chitré—plus climate information and weather forecasts, go to www.vgsbooks.com.

DAVID (population 100,000), the capital of Chiriquí Province, is the largest and most important city in western Panama. Gold prospectors founded the city in 1738. In modern times, David is a manufacturing center, renowned for leather products, such as saddles and harnesses. David is also home to food-processing and meat-packing companies.

The center of town is Cervantes Park, a spacious plaza. An art and history museum, located in a nineteenth-century mansion, exhibits religious art from Spanish times, Native American artifacts, and historic photographs. On the outskirts of David, visitors can bathe in hot sulfur springs, said to promote good health.

SANTIAGO (population 68,000) is the capital and principal town of Veraguas Province in central Panama. The city dates to Spanish times, when it prospered from mining and farming. The town has preserved many of its Spanish-era buildings. Taxis and pedestrians crowd Santiago's main street, Central Avenue, a bustling strip of shops, banks, hotels, and restaurants. The Pan American Highway runs directly through the center of town as well.

CHITRÉ (population 38,000), the capital of Herrera Province, sits about 90 miles (145 km) southwest of Panama City. Chitré's economy draws on nearby farms and ranches, whose owners buy and sell goods in town. The city also has some small food and beverage companies. The city's pride is an eighteenth-century cathedral (large church) that was extensively remodeled in 1988.

Chitré is also famous for its raucous festivals. Carnival, held during the four days before Ash Wednesday (a Christian holy day falling in February or March), is the occasion for parades and noisy outdoor parties. City residents hold the San Juan Batista Festival, celebrating the town's patron saint (protector), on June 24. Every October 19, residents honor the founding of Herrera Province.

HISTORY AND GOVERNMENT

The land of present-day Panama has been inhabited and traveled by Native Americans (also called Indians or indigenous people) for at least ten thousand years. Native peoples from South and Central America used Panama as a trading center, exchanging metal goods, gold jewelry, jade (a green gemstone), pottery, and silver with one another.

Two main indigenous groups, the Guaymí of western Panama and the Coclé of central Panama, lived near the present-day Panama Canal. The Kuna people, arriving in Panama about A.D. 1000 from northwestern South America, settled along the Caribbean coast and on the San Blas Islands. Smaller indigenous groups included the Térrabas, Talamancas, Cabegaras, Changuenas, and Dorasques. No single group controlled the entire isthmus. People lived in small independent villages, each ruled by a cacique.

The indigenous people of Panama lived by hunting animals, gathering edible plants and fruits, and growing corn, cacao, and root crops. They lived in small huts made of palm leaves and branches. They slept

in hammocks slung between the walls of their huts. They traded pottery, gold jewelry, and other goods with larger indigenous civilizations, including the Aztecs of present-day Mexico to the north. Canoes made from tree trunks allowed them to travel on rivers and along the coasts. A network of footpaths linked villages to one another and to trading centers on the coasts.

The European Conquest

In the fifteenth century, European explorers sailed west across the Atlantic Ocean, in search of unknown lands and an ocean passage to Asia. In 1492 Genoan navigator Christopher Columbus, sailing on behalf of Spain, landed in the West Indies, islands in the Caribbean Sea. In 1501 Spanish explorers Rodrigo de Bastidas, Juan de la Cosa, and Vasco Núñez de Balboa sailed from Spain to the northern coast of South America, then to the Caribbean coast of Panama.

Christopher Columbus was one of several Europeans to lead expeditions to the Caribbean coast of Central America in the early sixteenth century.

In 1502, on his fourth and final voyage to the Caribbean, Columbus landed in the Darién region. His crew raided Indian settlements for their jewelry and gold and built a small village along the coast. After Columbus left the region, however, the indigenous people killed many of the European pioneers. Others died of disease, and the settlement soon disappeared.

In 1510 a group of Spaniards again attempted to settle the Caribbean coast. These colonists had come to Central America seeking gold and silver. They also wanted to spread their religion, Catholicism (a form of Christianity), among the native inhabitants. To take control of the region, the colonists attacked the indigenous peoples of Panama. The colonists killed or drove away caciques in order to weaken native villages. The Spanish also kidnapped Indian men and women and used or sold them as slaves. The violence prompted many native people to flee inland, away from the seacoasts, and west to Costa Rica.

The first Spanish settlements on the Caribbean coast were Darién, Nombre de Dios, and Portobelo. These settlements struggled for years with limited food and resources. Because clearing the region's dense forests was difficult, most settlers in Panama could not grow enough crops to feed themselves. The settlers had also hoped—but failed—to find gold in Panama. They soon learned that the native people traded for their gold from South American tribes (although Panama did have what were then undiscovered gold deposits). Hungry and discouraged, many settlers died or abandoned their homes within a few years.

In 1513 Vasco Núñez de Balboa, leader of the colony at Darién, led an expedition across the Isthmus of Panama on foot. He became the first European to see the eastern shores of the Pacific Ocean. Spanish leaders realized that Panama was an important stepping-stone to the Pacific Ocean and to trade with Asia. To entice Spaniards to settle in Panama, the Spanish called the area Castilla del Oro, or Golden Castile, after the kingdom of Castile of medieval Spain.

The Spanish king appointed Pedro Arias de Ávila as governor of Castilla del Oro. But during de Ávila's reign, colonists broke into rival factions and fought over natural resources and control of gold and silver taken from the Indians.

For indigenous people, de Ávila's rule was especially harsh. He had his soldiers massacre thousands of Indians and destroy entire villages. At the same time, Indians died from diseases such as smallpox and measles, which colonists had brought from Europe. The Indians had no immunity, or natural resistance, to these diseases, and they died in great numbers. Those Indians who managed to survive the European onslaught of violence and disease fled from coastal areas into the mountainous interior.

In 1519 de Ávila founded Panama City on the Pacific coast. It flourished as a slave market, where landowners bought black captives from Africa, then forced them to work on their estates. Wealthy merchants built large mansions in the town, and skilled carpenters created a fine Catholic cathedral.

Panama City served as a staging ground for further explorations throughout Central and South America. After defeating the Inca people of Peru in the 1530s, Spanish conquistadors (conquerors) carried Inca treasures north along the Camino Real, or Royal Road, to Panama City. They sent the goods across the isthmus to Nombre de Dios on the Caribbean coast. From there, the treasures traveled by ship back to Spain.

FINDING SHIPS

History lives off the coasts of Panama in the form of sunken ships that lie underneath the coastal waters. In November 2001, divers discovered a ship named the *Vizcaina* off the Caribbean coast. This ship was one of four vessels from Christopher Columbus's final expedition to the Americas in 1502–1504.

Another spectacular find occurred just six months later, in May 2002. Scientists exploring the Pacific coastal waters discovered the *San Jose*, which ran aground and sank on June 17, 1631, in the Pearl Islands. The ship had left Peru carrying about 700 tons (635 metric tons) of gold and silver. Its cargo was bound for Spain via Panama's overland route to the Caribbean coast.

Piracy and Decline

After its conquest of the Caribbean region, Spain had to defend the territory against pirates and privateers from Great Britain and other parts of Europe. Privateering—attacking and looting enemy ships with government permission—was one way for Spain's enemies, including England, to weaken Spanish control in the Americas. Panama's coastal defenses were no match for the well-armed fleets of privateers that sailed up and down the coast to burn settlements, kill colonists, loot storehouses and treasure vaults, and drive the survivors away.

In 1572 the English privateer Sir Francis Drake attacked the Caribbean port of Nombre de Dios, easily overwhelming the city's defenses. Other small Caribbean settlements withered away as their inhabitants fell victim to privateers, hunger, raids by Indians and escaped black slaves, and disease.

In 1668 the daring English pirate Henry Morgan attacked Portobelo, capturing the town's fortress and looting its treasury. Morgan landed at Fort San Lorenzo in 1671. His troops captured the fort, then made their way along the Chagres River. With a force of about 1,200 men, Morgan attacked and burned Panama City. After this attack, residents founded a new and more heavily defended city a few miles to the east.

As the piracy continued, gold and slave traders began to avoid Panama. The area grew poor and isolated. In addition, rather than

Henry Morgan destroyed Panama City in 1671.

shipping cargo overland across the isthmus, the Spanish began to send more goods by ship around Cape Horn at the tip of South America. As trade decreased, many Panamanian families moved away to more promising places in Central and South America.

From 1799 to 1804, Alexander von Humboldt, a renowned German naturalist and explorer, traveled in South and Central America. By then, Europeans were busily trading with Asia but still contending with the long and dangerous route around Cape Horn. Navigators and merchants suggested the building of a canal somewhere in Central America to shorten the journey. Humboldt believed that the best place for such a canal was across southern Nicaragua, north of Costa Rica. Most geologists and engineers agreed, since the route across Nicaragua did not have to cross as many mountains. But others argued that a canal across Panama, running a shorter distance, would be better.

Independence

By the early 1800s, many Latin American colonists—inspired by the Revolutionary War in North America—were demanding greater liberty from Spain. They wanted control over their own resources and an end to the harsh rule of Spanish governors. The king of Spain sent his forces to put down this independence movement. In response, the colonists organized their own armies, formed legislatures, and wrote new constitutions. Fighting occurred throughout Central and South America.

In 1819, after a hard-fought struggle, Colombia won its independence from Spain. Two years later, Panama also declared its independence and joined a nation called Gran Colombia, which included modern-day Colombia, Venezuela, and Ecuador. The nation's first president was Simon Bolívar, a revolutionary who had led the fight against Spain. In

A FAILED UTOPIA IN PANAMA

In 1699 a Scotsman named William Paterson founded a colony in Panama's Darién region. At the time, Scotland was controlled by England. Paterson wanted to found a colony that would be totally independent of English rule. He also dreamed of opening a "free trade" route across the isthmus, independent of control by European governments, whether English, French, or Spanish. In honor of their home country, Paterson's settlers named the bay where they landed Caledonia Bay (*Caledonia* is Latin for Scotland). But the colonists died in great numbers from hunger and disease, and the colony was soon abandoned. Paterson himself barely survived to struggle back to the English colonies in North America.

1830 Ecuador and Venezuela seceded (withdrew) from Gran Colombia, but Panama remained a Colombian province.

In the late 1840s, prospectors discovered gold in California in the western United States. Thousands of hopeful miners from the eastern United States flocked to California. It was not an easy journey, however, as thousands of miles of plains, deserts, and mountain ranges lay between the eastern states and California. To avoid the dangerous overland journey, many miners tried a sea route. Some sailed around stormy Cape Horn. Others sailed to the Caribbean Sea, landing in Panama and then trekking through the mountains and rain forests of the isthmus to reach the Pacific coast.

To ease the overland journey across the isthmus, U.S. engineers began planning a railroad. The U.S.-based Panama Railroad Company began construction of the Panama Railroad in 1850 and completed the project in 1855. To build the railroad, the company hired thousands of black workers, descendants of African slaves, from islands in the Caribbean Sea. These workers settled in small towns along the railway route. They brought their own religious beliefs, languages, and culture to Panama. But they remained segregated (separated) from Panamanian and U.S. workers and were paid less for their labor.

In 1879 a French engineer named Ferdinand de Lesseps (builder of the Suez Canal in Egypt) started planning for a canal across Panama at its narrowest point. Lesseps wanted to build the canal at sea level by cutting through the mountains of central Panama. His workers began construction in 1882. But the sheer amount of earth to be moved, as well as diseases such as malaria and yellow fever that raged among the laborers, slowed construction. The French stopped their work in 1889, and Lesseps's company soon went bankrupt.

A MAN AND A HAT IN PANAMA

Ferdinand de Lesseps, the French engineer who first tried to build the Panama Canal, wore a light-colored straw hat to shield his bald head from the sun. When photographs of Lesseps appeared in newspapers all over the world, men living far from Panama began wearing similar hats, called Panama hats. Panama hats remain popular in tropical countries. But they are not made in Panama. Most are actually made in the South American nation of Ecuador.

The United States Steps In

Although several engineers in the United States still favored a canal across southern Nicaragua, eventually the U.S. government gave its support to a canal across Panama,

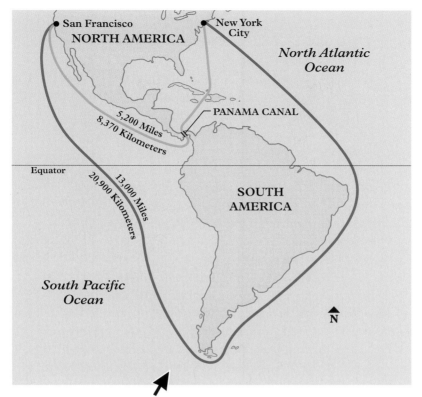

The United States was interested in building a canal in Panama because it would **significantly shorten the trip** from the Atlantic Ocean to the Pacific Ocean.

completing the work begun by Ferdinand de Lesseps. The U.S. engineers realized the difficulties of cutting through mountains to build a sea-level canal. Instead, they devised a system that would move boats from sea level to a higher elevation and then down again at the other end of the canal. They planned a series of locks that would fill with water to bring ships from sea level up to canal level and release water to bring the ships back down.

In the meantime, political turmoil boiled over in Colombia. Colombian coffee growers, angered by government policies, staged a rebellion called the War of the Thousand Days (1899–1902). When it was over, Colombia's government was too weak to fight an independence movement that was growing in Panama.

In 1903 the United States and Colombia negotiated a treaty. The United States offered Colombia $10 million in exchange for the rights to build the Panama Canal. The United States also wanted a one-hundred-year lease (rental agreement) on a 10-mile-wide (16-km-wide) Canal Zone, the area through which the canal would pass. This lease would allow the United States to operate and control the canal. The way seemed clear for construction. However, the Colombian legislature rejected the treaty.

Many Colombian lawmakers thought the United States was offering too little money.

In November 1903, Panamanian leaders declared their country's independence from Colombia. The United States, hoping to negotiate a canal treaty with a new Panamanian government, encouraged the independence movement. Colombia sent in troops to put down the Panamanian uprising, but the United States also sent troops to stop the Colombians. With U.S. help, the Panamanian rebels easily succeeded in throwing off Colombian rule. Soon afterward, the United States recognized Panama as an independent nation.

The United States then negotiated a canal treaty with Panama. Named the Hay-Bunau-Varilla Treaty, the agreement leased the Canal Zone directly to the United States, in exchange for a payment of $10 million. For the privilege of operating the canal, the United States would pay Panama an annual rent of $250,000. The treaty also gave the United States sovereign rights in Panama—the right to control Panama's affairs as if Panama were a colony of the United States.

In 1904 Panama created a constitution, modeled largely on the U.S. Constitution. According to the Panamanian constitution, the new Panamanian government would be headed by an elected president and a National Assembly, or legislature. The new government did not treat everyone equally, however. Women, blacks, and indigenous people were not considered citizens and did not have the right to vote. The constitution also granted the United States further control over Panama's affairs, such as the right to send soldiers to maintain order in Panama.

Building the Canal

In 1906 engineers and laborers arrived from the United States to complete the canal construction started by Ferdinand de Lesseps. Using huge steam shovels and working in blistering heat and humidity, construction workers gouged vast loads of dirt and rock from mountains lining the canal route. They loaded this "spoil" into train cars, which carried it to the coasts for disposal. The workers dug across rivers and lakes and dammed the Chagres River to create Gatun Lake. They built three massive concrete locks at each end of the canal to raise ships to canal level and lower them back to sea level.

The most serious hazards workers faced were malaria and yellow fever, diseases carried by the region's many mosquitoes. To combat

This photo shows the slow progress of **canal construction** in 1906. Construction workers removed 211 million cubic yards (161 million cubic m) of earth over the course of the canal construction. For further information and more photos of the canal and its construction, visit the links at www.vgsbooks.com.

these illnesses, which killed thousands of workers in the early years of construction, the United States sent William Gorgas, the head of the U.S. Army Medical Corps, to improve sanitation and living conditions. Gorgas drained stagnant water where mosquitoes bred, placed mosquito netting over doors and windows, and installed sewers and drainage systems. By the end of the canal's construction, the rates of infection from both malaria and yellow fever had declined dramatically.

The Panama Canal opened for business in 1914. On August 15, 1914, the *Ancon*, a ship owned by the Panama Railroad, became the first ship to complete the full trip through the canal. Ships from all over the world soon followed.

As more and more ships began using the canal, Panama saw great economic benefits. It collected rent on the Canal Zone from the United States, and Panamanian businesses flourished along the borders of the Canal Zone. The nation's economy grew rapidly, and the Panamanian government was able to build new roads, schools, and railroads. Farming, logging, and ranching also flourished in the countryside, and settlers cleared the wilderness for new towns.

U.S. Influence

Within the Canal Zone, the United States had full control. It built military bases and established a police force. Only U.S.-owned businesses were allowed to operate in the zone, and only canal workers were allowed to live there. Residents of the zone used U.S. money, attended U.S.-run schools, and used U.S. post offices. English was widely spoken inside the zone. A U.S. business called the Panama Canal Company was in charge of running the canal. A U.S. governor administered the zone.

The Canal Zone workforce included U.S. citizens (primarily white), both white and black Panamanians, and black workers recruited from

The **Gorgona School for Whites** was one of the segregated public schools operated for the children of U.S. citizens working in the Canal Zone.

Caribbean nations. But zone administrators kept the Panamanian and Caribbean workers segregated from the U.S. workers. The Panamanian and Caribbean natives attended separate schools, shopped in separate stores, used different hospitals, and lived in different housing facilities than the U.S. workers did. Panamanian and Caribbean workers were also paid less than U.S. workers. Panamanian and Caribbean workers resented the segregation and discrimination but had no power to make changes.

In addition to the Panama Canal Company, many other U.S. companies also set up business in Panama. The United Fruit Company built banana plantations (large farms) in the Panamanian countryside, then shipped its bananas to customers in the United States and Europe. United Fruit's "Great White Fleet" of ships, painted white to reflect the rays of the hot sun, sailed regularly from Colón and other ports.

As the largest investor in the Panamanian economy, the United States held great influence over Panama's politicians and elected governments. The United States intervened several times in Panamanian politics in the early decades of the twentieth century. For instance, in October 1925, tenants (people who rent their homes and apartments) revolted in Panama City. The tenants were angry about high rents and poor living conditions. Since the Panamanian constitution allowed the United States to maintain order in Panama, the Panamanian government invited the U.S. Army to put down the revolt. U.S. troops arrived on October 12, restored order, and left the country on October 23.

Panamanians grew increasingly unhappy with this kind of interference from the United States. They began to oppose U.S. domination of their political and economic life. In 1931 a group called Common

Action rose to power under the brothers Harmodio and Arnulfo Arias Madrid. Harmodio was elected president in 1932. The Arias brothers and their supporters protested U.S. domination of Panama. They also opposed the Panamanian oligarchy—a powerful group of businesspeople and landowners—that controlled Panama's government. Throughout Panama, support grew for a new canal treaty that would better compensate Panama for the use of its territory.

Seeking to avoid conflict in the Canal Zone, the United States agreed to negotiate, and in 1936 Panama and the United States signed the Hull-Alfaro Treaty. By this agreement, the annual rent paid by the United States increased to $430,000. Panamanian businesses also won the right to operate in the Canal Zone, and the United States lost its right to directly intervene in Panama's political conflicts.

Trouble in Government

In 1940 Panamanians elected Arnulfo Arias Madrid as president. In 1941 he revised the nation's constitution. The new constitution extended the presidential term from four to six years to increase presidential power. It also gave women the right to vote.

Arias Madrid claimed to stand for poor and working-class people against Panama's oligarchy and the United States. But he also appealed to racism and xenophobia (fear of foreigners) within Panama. His new constitution decreed that advertisements had to be printed and broadcast in Spanish, not English. The constitution also banned immigration by blacks into Panama and restricted the rights of blacks already living in Panama.

The United States was preparing for World War II (1939–1945), which had begun in Europe. Although the United States did not enter the war at first, it did worry about protecting its ships and the canal from attack. To protect sea traffic, the United States built more than one hundred military bases in Panama. This increased U.S.

BLACKS IN PANAMA

Just as blacks suffered discrimination inside the Canal Zone, they were also treated unjustly in other parts of Panama. Blacks of Caribbean descent generally spoke English and belonged to Protestant churches, which set them apart from the majority Spanish-speaking, Catholic Panamanians. Most blacks settled in separate black neighborhoods in large cities. Other Panamanians looked down on them as outsiders. The situation began to improve as younger generations of blacks, born in Panama, assimilated (blended) into the country's cultural and economic mainstream.

presence angered President Arias Madrid, and tensions with the United States grew. But Arias Madrid was unpopular with his own government as well. In 1941 his opponents staged a coup (revolt) that forced him out of office. The coup leaders replaced Arias Madrid with Ricardo Adolfo de la Guardia, a president more favorable to the United States. Both the United States and Panama officially entered World War II on the side of the Allies in December 1941.

Arnulfo Arias Madrid

In 1945 Enrique Jiménez succeeded de la Guardia as president. In the same year, the Panamanian legislature struck down the Arias Madrid constitution. A new constitution, passed in 1946, restored the four-year presidential term.

Arnulfo Arias Madrid returned to run for election against Domingo Díaz Arosemena in 1948. Each leader charged the other with fraud. José Antonio Remón Cantera, head of the national police force, threw his support to Arosemena, who then won the election. When Arosemena died the next year, Arias Madrid staged a coup, seized the presidency, and restored his 1941 constitution.

Arias Madrid again tried to increase his own power. In 1950 he tried to ban the right of habeas corpus—the right of an arrested citizen to argue the legality of his or her arrest before a judge. Fearing that Arias Madrid was striving to make himself a dictator, the legislature impeached (removed) him in 1951. Remón Cantera succeeded Arias Madrid and then won the 1952 elections. During Remón Cantera's term, Panama established a military-style police force, called the National Guard.

Turmoil in the Canal Zone

Under President Remón Cantera's urging, the United States agreed to revise the canal treaty again in 1955. Called the Eisenhower-Remón Treaty, the new agreement raised the annual rent on the Canal Zone to $1.93 million. It also equalized wages between U.S. and Panamanian citizens in the Canal Zone.

Blacks in the Canal Zone still suffered discrimination, however. They demonstrated for better housing and integrated (racially mixed) schools. Several times, these demonstrations erupted into violence. To solve this problem, which at times threatened canal operations, U.S. administrators simply deported blacks from the Canal Zone altogether, forcing black workers to resettle in Colón and Panama City.

Despite the Eisenhower-Remón Treaty, Panamanians still felt cheated by U.S. control over the canal. Panama's government wanted to share in the canal's profits, which were several times higher than the rent paid by the United States to operate the canal. Since the canal lay within Panama, Panamanians thought it rightly belonged to them. Several times in the late 1950s, Panamanians demonstrated against the United States and clashed with U.S. troops stationed in Panama.

In 1960 Panamanians demanded that their nation's flag fly in the Canal Zone beside the flag of the United States. The United States agreed to fly the flag but in just one place. In January 1964, when some U.S. schoolchildren refused to raise the Panamanian flag alongside the U.S. flag, Panamanians rioted. The riots resulted in more than twenty deaths.

The unrest disrupted trade and stability in the Canal Zone, convincing the United States that it had to make more concessions. The two nations agreed to negotiate a new canal treaty that would eventually turn over control of the canal and the Canal Zone to Panama.

The Torrijos Era

Arnulfo Arias Madrid won the presidential election again in 1968. But he was not popular with many National Guard officers, who suspected that he would fire all those who opposed his policies. Eleven days after the election, two officers, Major Boris Martinez and Colonel Omar Torrijos Herrera, forced the new president out of office. Torrijos then formed a junta (ruling council) of guard officers and named himself the country's new ruler. He ruled as a dictator, allowing no public opposition to his policies. Torrijos dissolved the National Assembly and banned all political parties. He would not allow Panamanian newspapers to write anything negative about the government. People could not gather in public to express their political opinions.

Despite his harsh rule, Torrijos gained the support of many Panamanian farmers for instituting land reform. That is, the government broke up large estates and turned small parcels of land over to ordinary farmers. Torrijos also improved Panama's schools, health-care facilities, and public works such as roads and bridges. He extended civil rights, giving blacks the right to vote and attend public schools. Torrijos also built up Panama's offshore banking industry. Offshore banking allowed foreign companies to bank in Panama without having to pay taxes and fees in their home countries.

Jimmy Carter *(left)* and Omar Torrijos shake hands after signing a new Panama Canal treaty in September 1977.

In 1972 the Torrijos junta changed the constitution, giving Torrijos more power. The constitution also gave indigenous people the right to vote. Torrijos then selected a new National Assembly, made up entirely of his supporters.

The next year, the Torrijos government began negotiating with the United States. President Jimmy Carter and Torrijos signed two new canal treaties in September 1977. Under the agreements, Panama would take control of the Canal Zone in 1979 and the canal itself in 1999. Panama would also operate eleven military bases formerly run by the United States. A Panama Canal Commission, run by Panamanians, would replace the Panama Canal Company. The United States and Panama also agreed to the canal's permanent neutrality—not taking sides in time of war. This provision would make sure that ships could still travel through the canal in wartime. The United States still held the right to intervene militarily, if necessary, to keep the canal open.

In October 1978, Torrijos resigned as head of Panama's government but remained commander of the National Guard. The new government was fairer. It restored many of the rights taken away in 1968. Political parties were again allowed to operate. The National Assembly then chose Arístides Royo Sánchez as the new president, to hold a six-year term. The next year, the United States turned over control of the Canal Zone to Panama.

The Rise and Fall of Manuel Noriega

In the early 1980s, Panama's economy struggled. The government spent more money than it took in, causing large budget shortfalls. Industry and farming slowed, and unemployment was high. Political conflict continued between the government and the National Guard. In 1983 an officer named Manuel Noriega emerged as the head of the Panamanian Defense Forces (PDF), the new name of the National Guard. Using the threat of a coup, Noriega pressured President Nicolás Ardito Barletta to resign in September 1985. Vice President Eric Arturo Delvalle replaced Ardito.

Noriega's opponents accused him of having orchestrated the death of Omar Torrijos in a plane crash in 1981. They also accused him of drug trafficking—arranging the illegal buying and selling of drugs— between Colombia and the United States. When the U.S. Senate demanded an investigation into these allegations, demonstrations and violence broke out in the streets of Panama City. A large crowd, rallied by Noriega's forces, attacked the U.S. Embassy there. The United States responded by breaking off economic ties with Panama.

Manuel Noriega

In February 1988, the U.S. government formally charged Noriega with drug trafficking. President Delvalle attempted to fire him. In response, Noriega forced Delvalle out of office and replaced him with Manuel Solís Palma. The United States still recognized Delvalle as head of the Panamanian government, setting the stage for a U.S. showdown with Noriega.

In December 1989, Noriega canceled the upcoming presidential election and had himself declared head of Panama's government. Noriega also declared that Panama was in a state of war with the United States. On December 20, the United States invaded Panama with twelve thousand troops, destroying PDF headquarters and capturing Noriega.

The United States resumed economic aid and diplomatic relations with Panama and brought Noriega to the United States. Noriega was tried by a U.S. federal court in Miami, Florida, and convicted of drug trafficking and money laundering (using money gained from criminal activity). He was sentenced to forty years in jail.

Mireya Elisa Moscoso Rodríguez was the first female president of Panama. She served from 1999 through 2004.

New Beginnings

In February 1990, Panama formed a new, seventy-two-member Legislative Assembly. Threatened by the PDF, the legislature abolished that organization and created a new civilian police force, coast guard, and air service.

Ernesto Pérez Balladares of the Revolutionary Democratic Party won the elections of May 1994. (One of his opponents was popular musician and actor Rubén Blades, who came in third in the voting.) In 1999 Mireya Elisa Moscoso Rodríguez—the widow of President Arnulfo Arias Madrid—won the presidency. She was the first woman to hold this office in Panama's history. That same year, as stipulated in the 1977 canal treaty, the United States turned over the canal to Panama.

Voters expected the country to prosper with the canal in their own hands, and they had high hopes for Moscoso. But the economy slowed, and unemployment grew during her term. The situation worsened after the September 11, 2001, terrorist hijackings in the United States. Tourists fearful of additional hijackings avoided air travel. Fears of terrorism also caused a worldwide business slowdown, which reduced the number of ships passing through the canal.

Moscoso ran for reelection in 2004 but lost to Martín Torrijos, the son of former president Omar Torrijos. Although his father had ruled as a dictator, the younger Torrijos promised to distance himself from the abuses of the past. Upon taking office, he vowed to fight corruption and the unequal distribution of wealth in Panama.

Government

Panama is divided into nine provinces: Bocas del Toro, Chiriquí, Coclé, Colón, Darién, Herrera, Los Santos, Panama, and Veraguas. The president appoints the governors of these provinces. The San Blas Islands are an indigenous territory, governed by the Kuna Indians who live there. The Kuna General Congress passes laws and regulations for the territory, and the Kuna send elected representatives to the Panamanian government.

An elected seventy-two-member Legislative Assembly, which sits for two four-month sessions every year, makes laws that govern the nation. People in rural areas vote for their representatives directly. Candidates receiving the most votes win seats in the legislature. But people in urban areas elect their representatives by voting for political parties. Parties gaining the most votes in the election can send the most members to the legislature (a practice intended to prevent a single person from getting too much power). The vote for the legislature takes place every five years.

People vote directly for the president, in elections held once every five years. They also vote for first and second vice presidents, who assist the president. The president appoints a cabinet, a board of twelve ministers who run various government departments, such as the Ministry of Health. The president can veto (reject) laws passed by the legislature, but the legislature can override a veto by voting against it with a two-thirds majority.

By law, all citizens aged eighteen and older must vote, but in practice, many Panamanians avoid this duty. Because the military has interfered in elections many times in the past, members of the armed forces are not allowed to run for office or publicly support any candidate or political party.

The highest court in Panama is the Supreme Court of Justice. It consists of nine judges, who serve ten-year terms. Five superior courts deal with important civil and criminal cases. Citizens can appeal decisions (ask for reviews) of the lower courts at three courts of appeal. Eighteen circuit courts deal with less serious criminal matters and lawsuits. Local judges handle minor crimes.

Visit www.vgsbooks.com where you can find links to the most up-to-date population figures, government information, current headlines, interesting facts, customs, and photographs from Panama.

THE PEOPLE

Panama has a population of more than 3 million, with a population density of about 103 people per square mile (40 people per sq. km). The former Canal Zone, with large urban areas at both ends, has the highest population density. The most sparsely populated regions are Darién and the mountainous regions of western Panama. Overall, Panama's population is 62 percent urban, 38 percent rural.

Ethnic Groups

Panama's people fall into several racial and ethnic groups. Indigenous tribes were the original inhabitants of Panama. They once lived by hunting animals and gathering edible plants and fruits. As more and more Europeans arrived, the native people began to suffer. European settlers attacked indigenous villages, killing many caciques and enslaving their followers. Many native people died of diseases brought from Europe. When European settlers built ranches and cleared forests, some native wildlife

died out, leaving fewer animals to hunt. Traditional indigenous lifestyles began to disappear.

In modern times, Native Americans make up about 5 percent of Panama's population. The largest group is the Guaymí, who live in western Panama, Bocas del Toro, Chiriquí, and Veraguas provinces. The Guaymí still make a living as farmers. Some raise crops such as manioc (an edible root), corn, sugarcane, and tobacco on their own land. Other Guaymí farmers can't afford their own land. They work as laborers on large banana and coffee plantations.

The Kuna people are concentrated in the San Blas Islands. In the early years of independence, the Kuna fought to govern the islands themselves, independent of the Panamanian government. They won this right in 1925 and since then have elected their own legislative council to govern their *comarca* (territory). On the islands, the modern Kuna live by hosting tourists, growing coconuts, and fishing. Other Indians in Panama, including the Coclé of central Panama, live by farming and selling craft items.

People of **varied ethnic backgrounds** crowd the streets in Panama City.

 Visit www.vgsbooks.com for links to websites with additional information about the customs and lifestyles of Panama's native peoples, including the Guaymí people in western Panama and the Kuna people on the San Blas Islands.

When the Spanish arrived in Panama, many of them intermarried with native people. Their descendants, people of mixed race, are called mestizos. They make up 70 percent of Panama's population. Criollos are descendants of Spaniards who did not intermarry with native peoples. This group makes up about 10 percent of the Panamanian population. Criollo families traditionally held the most economic and political power in Panama.

Blacks make up about 13 percent of the population. Some are descended

In 1985 the Kuna Indians established the Kuna Wildlife Project, a 148,000-acre (60,000-hectare) rain forest preserve along the Caribbean coast. It is the first nature preserve established by indigenous people in the Americas.

from slaves imported from Africa when Panama was a Spanish colony. The rest descend from West Indian blacks (also descendants of slaves) who once helped build the Panama Railroad and the Panama Canal or worked on the country's banana plantations. Most black Panamanians live in Panama City or Colón, the largest urban areas. There are also small black communities in towns along the Atlantic coast and in the more isolated region of Darién. Blacks attained citizenship and the right to vote during the Torrijos administration.

People of East Indian, Chinese, Middle Eastern, and European heritage also live in modern-day Panama. Many of their ancestors arrived in Panama in the late nineteenth century. Many families from the United States, once employed in the Canal Zone, have remained in Panama after the handover of the canal.

Health and Welfare

Panama's annual population growth rate is 1.3 percent. The nation's population is expected to reach 4.2 million by the year 2025. Infant mortality—the number of infants who die around the time of childbirth—stands at 21 deaths per 1,000 live births. Panama's fertility rate, the number of babies born to each woman, is 2.5. Life expectancy is 70 years for men and 74 years for women—slightly better than the average rate for Central America.

During the twentieth century, Panama established good health-care facilities. Income from the Panama Canal allowed Panama to build sewers, water treatment systems, hospitals, and clinics. The Torrijos government also sponsored new water and sewer projects, health education programs, and health clinics. Panama vaccinates (protects against a disease) more than 90 percent of its young people each year against measles and tuberculosis.

This poster encourages Panamanians to **vaccinate** their children.

Despite generally good health care in Panama, some rural areas lag far behind. In particular, indigenous people have worse health, due to a less healthy and varied diet, and less access to medicines, clean drinking water, and health facilities than other Panamanians.

Panama has a relatively high rate of HIV infection (HIV, or human immunodeficiency virus, causes acquired immuno-deficiency syndrome, or AIDS). The rate stands at 1.5 percent for the people ages 15 through 49. Only Honduras, with a rate of 1.6 percent, has a higher rate in the region. About twenty-five thousand Panamanians are living with HIV, with a growing number of women and children becoming infected. The government has stepped up education about HIV/AIDS prevention in rural areas and among the urban poor, where infection rates are growing fastest.

> **Because the midday sun can be searing hot in Panama, many people rise with the sun and carry out their work early in the morning. They take a long break for lunch and a siesta (nap) in the hottest part of the day before returning to work again.**

Malaria, spread by the bite of the anopheles mosquito, was once widespread in Panama. By using pesticides and draining stagnant wetlands where mosquitoes breed, Panama has largely ended that disease in the Canal Zone and in cities. But malaria is still found in the Bocas del Toro, San Blas, and Darién regions. Rural Panamanians also suffer from yellow fever and dengue, diseases also transmitted by mosquitoes. Cholera, transmitted by food or water that has been contaminated with human waste, is another disease found in rural Panama. In rainy seasons, some people get hantavirus, a dangerous illness spread from rodents to humans.

Women in Panama

Throughout most of the twentieth century, young women in Panama (as elsewhere in Latin America—the Spanish-speaking nations south of the United States) found themselves with fewer choices than men. Many girls got little or no formal education. They left school early to get married or to work in low-paying jobs to help support their families. In the early twentieth century, women were not allowed to attend universities, vote, or run for political office. In the mid-1900s, women who applied for jobs often had to pass a pregnancy test. Those found to be pregnant were not

allowed to work. In addition, many Panamanian women suffered from violence at the hands of their husbands. The authorities did not punish men for domestic violence.

In the 1990s, the situation changed for the better. In 1995 a new law made domestic violence a crime. In 1997 election laws were changed to require that at least 30 percent of all candidates for the legislature be women. For many Panamanians, the election of Mireya Moscoso as president in 1999 symbolized dramatic progress in women's rights.

But in the twenty-first century, women in Panama continue to suffer from inequality. The average female worker earns about half what the average male worker earns. Women earn less, in part, because they have less schooling. Only about 37 percent of teenage girls graduate from high school. Teen pregnancy also keeps women from achieving in Panama. Nearly 10 percent of girls between ages fifteen and nineteen get pregnant. A high percentage of these expectant mothers are jobless and live in poverty. Panama's Ministry of Health has started a sex education program in public schools in an attempt to combat teen pregnancy. It also distributes birth control devices through public health clinics.

Urban and Rural Life

In Panama, rural and urban life differ somewhat. Panamanian farmers and rural laborers live in small homes, many of them with only one or two rooms. Many homes near the seacoasts have roofs made of palm branches and walls made of sugarcane stalks. Rural dwellers shop at markets in towns and villages, where they can share news and strike up friendships. Many rural Panamanians attend church services regularly.

Homes made of sturdy branches and roofed with palm leaves, are common throughout rural Panama.

The cities of Panama are more diverse. Homes range from luxury apartments for the wealthy to shacks made of wood and tin for the poor. Middle-class families often live in one-story homes with white-washed walls, tile roofs, and small gardens or courtyards for privacy. During the evening, many people stroll through city streets and plazas, large central squares where families can socialize and young people can meet, talk, and flirt. Like rural Panamanians, many urban dwellers attend church regularly.

Education

Panama's public education system dates to independence in 1903. In the twentieth century, the government spent up to 25 percent of its budget building and fixing schools, buying equipment, and training teachers. By the turn of the twenty-first century, Panama had achieved the highest rate of literacy (a measure of people's ability to read and write) in Central America—93 percent for men, 92 percent for women. But while nearly all adults in cities can read and write, the literacy rate drops in rural areas. Only about half of indigenous people are literate.

In Panama, elementary and secondary (middle and high) schools each last six years. Public education is free. Secondary school classes include Spanish, social studies, religion, and art. About 90 percent of Panama's children attend primary school, while about 50 percent attend secondary school. Enrollment is generally higher in the cities than in rural areas, where many children quit school after the primary

Students work on their assignments in a classroom in Boquete, Panama.

level to take jobs. Many children from wealthy families attend private schools. Although these schools are expensive, they offer a good education and prepare students for university-level studies.

The University of Panama was established in 1935. Based in Panama City, the university also has six branches in smaller cities throughout the country. In 1965 the Catholic Church founded the University of Santa María la Antigua, also in Panama City. In 1975 the Engineering Department of the University of Panama became a separate school. Known as La Technologica, or the Technological University, this school offers bachelor's and master's degrees in sciences, engineering, computer programming, and related fields. Panama also has schools focusing on business management, hotel management, and tourism. Schools for disabled students include the National School for the Deaf and the Helen Keller School for the Blind in Panama City.

CULTURAL LIFE

Panama has a diverse cultural flavor. Its first traditions began with indigenous people. When Panama became a colony of Spain, it took on Spanish cultural traditions, such as the Catholic religion and the Spanish language. The arrival of workers from Africa, the Caribbean, Europe, and North America gave Panama an even more mixed and international outlook. After the country achieved independence in 1903, a new influence arrived from the United States, which owned the Panama Canal and dominated the Panamanian economy. Many twentieth-century Panamanian artists, writers, and musicians trained in Europe or North America, then brought foreign styles in art and music home to Panama. Coming full circle, many indigenous art forms have been revived in Panama.

● Music

Panama's complex musical traditions developed out of the country's kaleidoscope of ethnic groups, including indigenous, European,

African, and Caribbean peoples. The traditional couples' dance of Panama, the *tamborito* (little drum), involves a men's drum ensemble and female singers, and a circle of onlookers who clap their hands in time with the dancers. Another dance, the *mejorana,* is performed by rows of men and women facing each other and dancing to the music of a violin or singer. Mejorana songs are performed only by men, who accompany themselves on a kind of guitar.

Panama also has adopted the *cumbia,* a dance that came to Central America with early black immigrants. Traditionally, the cumbia is performed to the music of a violin or accordion and drums, but in modern times, cumbia bands have added brass instruments. In the 1960s and 1970s, Panamanian singer Rubén Blades helped popularize a musical style known as salsa. The style began in Colombia and then spread around the rest of Latin America and eventually to the United States.

Panamanian musicians play a variety of instruments. They use violins, accordions, and small guitars known as *mejoraneras.* Percussion

instruments include a variety of large and small drums, bean-filled gourds known as maracas, and the *guáchara*, a grooved gourd that the player scrapes with a small stick. The Kuna Indians play a set of seven small bamboo flutes known as the *kamu-purui*.

Panamanian musicians also play classical styles. The National Orchestra of Panama, established in 1952, performs the classical music of European composers. Panama's leading composers include Santos Jorge, who wrote Panama's national anthem, and Roque Cordero, who has written prize-winning symphonies and other classical works. Cordero studied with leading symphony conductors in the United States and has also served as director and conductor of the National Orchestra of Panama.

Language, Literature, and Communications

The indigenous tribes of Panama spoke a variety of languages before the arrival of the Spanish. These languages had no written form. Although many indigenous languages died out after the Spanish arrived, others survived, and many indigenous people still use them.

Members of the Kuna tribe use two different languages, depending on region. The Guaymí, Bribri, and other Native American groups also speak distinctive languages. In many places, people have mixed

indigenous languages with European languages to make new dialects (variations on a language). In the islands of Bocas del Toro, the local dialect of Guari-Guari mixes Guaymí, Spanish, and English.

European explorers and settlers spoke Spanish, which became the official language of Panama. The long presence of the United States in Panama has led to the use of English as well. About 25 percent of Panamanians know or use English in addition to Spanish. The descendants of immigrants from Jamaica, Trinidad, and other Caribbean islands sometimes use Creole, a mixture of English, Spanish, and French words. A small community of Caribbean blacks, descended from immigrants from the island of Saint Lucia, uses a variation of French. There are also small Chinese-speaking communities in Panama City and Colón.

Major Panamanian writers include Rogelio Sinán, Roque Javier Laurenza, and José de Jesús Martinez. Tristán Solarte was the pen name (fictitious name) of Guillermo Sánchez Borbón, who wrote acclaimed novels and poetry. In 1937 Solarte published *The Drowned Man*, the story of a young poet whose murder brings out many strange and unknown facts about his life. Solarte won literary awards for *Confessions of a Magistrate* and *The Guitarist*. In 1960 Joaquín Beleño wrote the English-language novel *Gamboa Road Gang*, about the struggles of Caribbean workers brought to Panama to work on the Panama Canal. Rosa Maria Britton is a contemporary writer known for her novels, plays, and short stories. Her work has been included in several story collections, including *When New Flowers Bloomed: Short Stories by Women Writers from Costa Rica and Panama.*

Panamanians follow politics and international events closely through newspapers, television, and radio. The major Panamanian newspapers, *Diario el Universal de Panama*, *La Prensa*, and *El Siglo*, are published in Panama City. An English-language newspaper, the *Panama News*, appeals to expatriates (people living abroad) from the United States, as well as tourists from North America.

Nearly every household in Panama owns at least one radio. Battery-powered radios bring news of the outside world to those communities without reliable electricity or daily newspapers. The nation's principal radio stations mix news with sports, music, and variety shows. Panama has four national television stations and a small film industry.

An Internet café in Panama City

In the early 2000s, Panama's Pearl Islands twice served as the location for the hit U.S. reality TV show *Survivor.*

Internet cafés have opened in Panama's large cities. The cafés offer customers inexpensive time on-line to check their e-mail, visit websites, and chat with friends around the globe. About 37 of every 1,000 households have a computer, while 164 per 1,000 have a telephone.

Arts and Crafts

Before the European conquest, native people made a variety of crafts, including baskets, pottery, jewelry, woodcarvings, and leather goods. Many traditional forms and designs have survived. In the cities, small companies mass-produce traditional-style crafts for sale. In the countryside, villagers commonly sell weaving, jewelry, pottery, and woodcarvings to tourists.

Women of the Kuna tribe make beautifully detailed cloth panels called *molas*, which were originally used to decorate their blouses. Molas include up to seven layers of colored cloth, with designs of fishes, birds, and other animals as well as abstract shapes showing through the upper layers.

Guamyi Indians use **chacaras** to carry their loads.

In the Darién region, the men of the Coclé tribe make woodcarvings from cocobolo, a hard, dense-grained wood. They use knives and files to fashion the shape, then polish the carvings to a deep shine. Coclé women create beaded arm bracelets known as *chaquiras.* The Coclé also make wood, silver, and stone replicas of ancient ornaments called *huacas.* These figurines were buried with tribal leaders in ancient times. Modern huacas depict crocodiles, jaguars, frogs, condors, or human warriors.

The Ngobe people of the Chiriquí region make *chacaras,* bags woven from the fiber of pineapple plants. The bags can stretch to many times their original size. People wear them on their backs, dangling from a narrow band looped around the head.

A Kuna woman displays brightly colored **molas.** If you would like to learn more about the arts and crafts of Panama, go to www.vgsbooks.com for links.

During colonial times, Panamanian artists made sculptures and paintings for churches and missions (large church complexes). The artists copied popular Spanish styles to make flowery altarpieces, woodcarvings, and sculpture. One of the most famous works of this period is the *Immaculate Conception,* a religious painting displayed in the cathedral in San Carlos.

After independence, President Manuel Amador Guerrero and the artist Roberto Lewis founded the National Academy of Painting in Panama City. It became the training school for the country's leading twentieth-century artists, including Eudoro Silvera, Juan Manuel Cedeño, and Isaac Leonardo Benítez.

A leading modern painter, Coqui Calderón, uses abstract forms and a rich palette of colors in her works, shown in many prominent galleries outside Panama. The Museum of Contemporary Art in Panama City showcases the work of other established and upcoming contemporary painters and sculptors.

Religion

The indigenous people of Panama practiced age-old religions. They used chants and rituals to ask the gods for a good harvest, cures for illness, or success in war. Many traditional rituals, songs, and beliefs have survived among the indigenous people of modern Panama. Some groups still use chants and rituals to heal the sick. Others perform ancient ritual dances to greet visitors.

Spanish conquerors were determined to make Panama a Catholic country like Spain. They converted native people to Catholicism, often by force. The Roman Catholic Church soon became the dominant church of Panama.

Since the 1960s, the Catholic Church has been heavily involved in helping poor, minority, and indigenous peoples in Panama. It has also fought for Panamanian ownership of the Panama Canal, protection of the environment, and other causes. In poor and rural areas, religious organizations called Christian Base Communities have helped local people build new schools, roads, clinics, and water systems. They have also helped the poor vote in elections and bring grievances to government officials.

In modern Panama, about 90 percent of the population is Catholic, although many people do not regularly attend church. Students in Panama's schools can take courses

Catholics celebrate Sunday Mass at **El Carmen Church in Panama City.** The majority of Panamanians are Catholic.

in religious history and doctrine, but these courses are not required. In some areas, Christian and indigenous beliefs mingle. For instance, the Kuna and the Ngobe peoples pray to Catholic saints, but in their version of worship, some of these saints take the form of traditional animal spirits.

The nation's constitution upholds freedom of religion, and some people belong to other faiths besides Catholicism. About 8 percent of Panama's people are Protestant (members of Christian churches distinct from the Catholic Church). Panama has attracted immigrants from the Middle East, Europe, and Asia, and they have brought different religions to Panama. For instance, communities of Muslims, Jews, and Hindus are found in Panama City, together making up about 2 percent of the nation's population.

Festivals and Holidays

Panamanians enjoy a very busy calendar of national and religious holidays. National holidays include January 9, known as Martyr's Day, in which Panama honors those who fell in the struggle for independence. Labor Day (honoring workers) takes place on May 1, while August 15 marks the founding of the Republic of Panama in 1903. October 11 is Revolution Day, the day in 1968 when the National Guard overthrew a corrupt Panamanian government.

Many holidays fall in November. November 1 is National Anthem Day. On November 3, people celebrate Panama's independence from Colombia. November 10 is the First Call of Independence Day, celebrated by the people of Los Santos, the first city in Panama to demand independence from Spain in 1821. November 28 marks the independence of Colombia (then including the province of Panama) from Spain.

Important Catholic holidays include Good Friday and Easter in April or May, All Souls' Day on November 2, and Christmas on December 25. On December 8, Panama celebrates the Immaculate Conception, which honors the Virgin Mary, the mother of Jesus. This day is also observed as Mother's Day.

The Carnival season, a time of celebration in much of Latin America, begins the weekend before Ash Wednesday (the beginning of a period of forty days of penance before Easter). During Carnival, work

THE FRILLY POLLERA

The national dress for Panamanian women is the *pollera*, a long, ruffled skirt and an elaborate, hand-embroidered top. The pollera began as an everyday costume in seventeenth-century Spain and was later adopted by Panamanian colonists. The seamstresses of Los Santos Province are said to make Panama's finest polleras, which are worn in modern times only on Sundays and on special occasions.

Residents of Bocas del Toro Province celebrate **Carnival** with a water fight.

comes to a stop. People fill the streets for parades, singing, dancing, and celebrating. One of the largest Carnival festivals takes place in Las Tablas, a town southwest of Panama City. At the Las Tablas celebration, teams compete in a variety of sporting contests, as well as competition for the best costumes and best floats. In Panama City, citizens fill the streets for several days of parties, dancing, parades, and other merriment. In a famous Panama Carnival tradition, the *mojadera* (getting drenched) celebrants turn fire hoses, buckets of water, and water balloons on one another.

A popular event known as the Festival of the Black Christ takes place in Portobelo every October 21. The Black Christ, or El Nazareno, is a small, dark-skinned statue of Jesus that was found on the nearby shore by a fisher during the seventeenth century. According to legend, the statue miraculously ended a cholera epidemic that struck the city in 1821. During the Festival of the Black Christ, religious pilgrims from all over Panama arrive to follow a solemn parade of the statue through the city's streets.

◎ Sports and Recreation

In Panama, soccer is the favorite spectator and team sport. But many other sports are catching up in popularity. Panama has a small basketball league, and amateur baseball and softball teams compete in every

Cayucos are short, broad canoes, based on indigenous canoes, that hold four rowers. The Balboa Paddle Club holds four cayuco races each year. The most famous and popular is the **Ocean-to-Ocean Race**, first run in 1954. During this race, rowers follow the Panama Canal from the Atlantic to the Pacific, taking their boats out of the water and carrying them around the locks. The rowers cover a distance of about 43 miles (69 km) in three days.

city. Horse racing and greyhound racing bring out gamblers and spectators in Panama City.

Professional boxing draws many fans as well. Small gyms in Panama City and other towns train young Panamanian men, who see boxing as a means of escaping poverty. Panama has produced twenty world champions, most in the lighter weight classes. Roberto Duran, a world champion in several different weight classes in the 1970s and 1980s, has become a national hero.

Visitors to the country favor individual sports such as cycling, diving, sport fishing, and hiking. Surfers head for the big waves breaking off Santa Catalina Beach on the Azuero Peninsula. Coiba Island is a favorite with snorkelers and divers. In sheltered bays and coastal reefs, divers can explore the wrecks of old ships. Panama is also renowned for its deep-sea fishing. In Pinas Bay on the Pacific coast, anglers pull marlin, sailfish, yellowfin tuna, snapper, and other species from the deep ocean waters.

For links to various cultural websites where you'll find recipes, information on holidays and festivals, artwork, literature, and more, go to www.vgsbooks.com.

Foods of Panama

Panamanian cooking includes a full menu of beef, fish, and chicken dishes. A popular dish known as *sancocho* is a spicy stew of chicken and vegetables. Beef dishes include *ropa vieja,* or "old clothes." This dish consists of thinly sliced, cooked beef placed on a bed of rice or yucca (a fleshy fruit). *Casado* is a hearty beef dish prepared a bit differently in every household. The typical casado includes plantains, starchy fruits that resemble bananas, as well as rice and a vegetable such as cabbage or corn. *Carimañola* combines pork with fried yucca.

PLANTAIN TEMPTATION

Plantains are a favorite food in Panama. This sweet dessert is tasty and easy to make.

1 cup sugar

½ teaspoon vanilla

dash of cinnamon

1½ cups water

3 large ripe plantains (available at specialty groceries and some supermarkets)

1 tablespoon oil

1 tablespoon butter or margarine

1. In a mixing bowl, combine sugar, vanilla, cinnamon, and water and set aside.
2. Soften the plantains in their skins by hitting them on all sides with a wooden spoon.
3. Peel the plantains and cut them widthwise into 5 pieces each.
4. In a large skillet, melt oil and butter on medium-high heat.
5. Carefully add plantains and fry until brown, turning once.
6. Reduce heat to low and pour sugar mixture over plantains.
7. Continue cooking until the liquid thickens, about 15 minutes.
Serve hot.

Serves 4 to 5

Empanadas are another favorite in Panama. These are fried pastry turnovers filled with ground beef, onion, and chilis.

Seafood abounds in Panama's street markets and on dinner tables throughout the country. Shrimp, lobster, and squid are common foods in coastal areas, while people inland favor trout and other freshwater fish from rivers and streams. Seviche is a tangy preparation of ocean shellfish or freshwater fish, chopped into small pieces and soaked in lemon juice, then stirred with chopped celery, chopped onion, hot chilis, and spices.

Panamanians enjoy a wide variety of tropical fruit, with papayas, bananas, coconuts, and mangoes among the most popular. Plantains are a common ingredient in Panamanian cooking. They can be eaten salted and fried or baked in brown sugar. Favorite beverages include strong coffee, coconut milk, fruit drinks, and carbonated soft drinks. Many street vendors offer a syrupy ice dessert known as *raspado*. *Chicheme* is a popular drink made of mashed sweet corn, milk, honey, vanilla, and cinnamon.

THE ECONOMY

In the century since independence, Panama has benefited economically from the Panama Canal and its location as a shipping crossroads. While most Central American nations depended on farming for income, Panama profited from transportation, warehousing, international trade, and other businesses related to the canal. The country also developed a large banking sector, which attracted money and investment from all over the world.

But during the 1980s and 1990s, Panama's economy declined for several reasons. Traffic through the Panama Canal began to slow, as the canal is too small to accommodate new large supertankers and other large cargo ships. Panama also became a transfer point for illegal drugs moving from South and Central America to North America. When money from this smuggling began flowing through the banking system, Panama's reputation suffered. Foreign companies avoided doing business there. In 1988 the United States cut economic aid to Panama, which also hurt the economy.

As the economy faltered, Panama began to borrow money from foreign countries. The large amount of debt (money that needed to be paid back) hurt Panama's economy even more. The withdrawal of U.S. citizens after the handover of the Panama Canal also hurt Panama, because with fewer Americans, there were fewer well-off people to purchase Panamanian products.

Despite recent difficulties, Panama's economy is still strong. Since it was transferred to Panama's control on December 31, 1999, the Panama Canal has become one of the country's major moneymakers. The canal charges fees to each ship that passes through (large freighters can pay as much as $150,000 for using the canal). In 2002 the Panama Canal paid a total of $272 million into the country's treasury. Foreign investment has also made Panama one of the most prosperous countries in Latin America. In the early twenty-first century, Panama's GDP (gross domestic product—the total value of goods and services produced in Panama) had reached $17 billion annually, equal to $5,900 per person.

Nevertheless, many people in Panama are struggling. For example, about 40 percent of the population lives below the poverty line (a measure of poverty set by the government). The average annual salary of $6,000 is high by Central American standards, but in the big cities of Panama, this salary can barely sustain a family. The gap between rich and poor people is great in Panama. While the poorest 10 percent take home only 1.2 percent of the national income, the wealthiest 10 percent take home 35 percent of the total income.

Services

Service businesses such as banking, insurance, and tourism contribute about 76 percent of the GDP in Panama, a proportion higher than in any other Central American nation. Financial services, including banking and insurance, make up the most important part of the service sector. These businesses contribute about 15 percent of the GDP. Panama's banking policies are very attractive to foreign companies. Companies can use Panama's banks with a minimum of fees, taxes, and regulations. Another attraction for foreign companies is that Panama uses the U.S. dollar and the balboa as its official currency. Foreign companies like doing business in U.S. dollars, the most widely accepted currency in the world.

The banking district in Panama City, known as Paitilla, is full of skyscrapers.

Panama also boasts a busy ship registration business. This business allows foreign companies to register their ships in Panama and avoid paying higher fees and taxes in their home countries.

The tourism industry brings in money from foreign visitors. It also provides employment to thousands of hotel staff, wilderness guides, ship crews, and restaurant workers. Panama's wealth of natural attractions, including tropical rain forests, unspoiled coastlines, and the Darién region, draws adventurers from all over the world. The canal itself has become a popular tourist attraction. Many cruise ships take passengers through the canal.

But tourism is subject to political events within and outside Panama's borders. For instance, the September 11, 2001, terrorist attacks on the United States struck fear into many travelers. For several months afterward, tourists were reluctant to travel to foreign countries. Tourism-related businesses lost money.

Manufacturing

Manufacturing (including agricultural processing) accounts for about 17 percent of Panama's GDP. The manufacturing sector includes small factories that prepare canned fruit and vegetables, process sugar and coffee, and make cigarettes from tobacco. Panama also has small textile, metalworking, machinery, chemical, and oilrefining industries. Most manufacturing takes place in and along the former Canal Zone.

HOW TO CROSS THE PANAMA CANAL

A ship that needs to cross the Panama Canal must first request permission from canal operators by radio. At the canal entrance, a canal pilot boards the ship. The pilot's job is to run the ship through the canal.

The ship then enters a series of three concrete locks. These chambers fill with water to raise the ship to canal level, 85 feet (26 m) above sea level. Electric trains known as mules, which run on tracks alongside the locks, are attached to the ship by ropes. They help stabilize and guide the ship inside the locks.

After leaving the locks, the ship travels through the canal itself, including 163-square-mile (422-sq.-km) Gatun Lake. At the other end of the canal, the ship enters another series of three locks. This time, water flows out of the locks, lowering the ship back to sea level. The trip takes about eight hours.

For a link to a visual demonstration of how the locks work, visit www.vgsbooks.com.

Workers sew garments in a **clothes factory.** To learn more about Panama's economy, visit www.vgsbooks.com for links.

In recent years, competition with other nations in Latin America has challenged Panama's manufacturing sector. Laborers in poorer countries will work for lower salaries. So some Panamanian factories have moved abroad, to take advantage of cheaper labor costs.

Farming

Agriculture, including farming, forestry, and fishing contributes about 7 percent of Panama's GDP. About 8 percent of the nation's land is cultivated (farmed), with another 20 percent used as pasture.

In the 1980s, the government began controlling the prices of basic foods such as rice, potatoes, and meat. With the price of these

A small amount of Panama's land is used for **farming.** Here farmers harvest sod to be used for lawns of newly constructed buildings.

goods fixed, farmers found it more difficult to make a profit raising them. Growers made new investments in coconuts, cacao, coffee beans, corn, and tobacco. In the 1990s, farmers also increased the production of livestock, including cattle, pigs, and chickens.

Bananas are an important agricultural crop, and they make up the largest share of Panamanian exports. Many banana plantations are owned by the Chiriquí Land Company, which is in turn owned by a U.S. company, Chiquita Brands.

In 1979 Panama built a new fishing port at Vacamonte. This port expanded the fishing industry along the Pacific coast. Since then, Panama has become one of the world's leading exporters of shrimp. Seafood exports also include lobsters, anchovies, and herring.

Mining and Energy

Panama's mining sector has good potential. Large reserves of gold, silver, and copper exist in western Panama. But a complex mining law, passed in 1963, has discouraged new exploration and excavation. Outside of small coal mines in the Río Indio region, there were no mining operations in the early years of the twenty-first century. In 2003 the government proposed a new law to ease restrictions on mining.

Panama operates thermal energy plants, which capture the heat of underground water to create electricity. Panama's many rivers are also used to generate electricity. Hydroelectric plants such as the La Fortuna plant and the Río Esti Project on the Chiriquí River have enabled Panama to become self-sufficient in electricity production.

MINING IN PANAMA

Panama may hold large underground reserves of gold, copper, and silver, but controversy surrounds the mining industry. Foreign companies want Panama's government to make it easier to operate mines there. These companies complain that complex laws and regulations make it nearly impossible to explore and extract minerals from the earth.

But environmentalists have a different view of the subject. They point out that building mines damages forests. The chemicals used in mining also pollute the soil and water. Many indigenous tribes resist mining projects on their land. One of these tribes, the Ngobe-Buglé, is fighting the development of the huge Cerro Colorado mine, planned to exploit a large copper deposit in Chiriquí Province. Panamanian leaders, who see mining as a vital source of income for Panama in the future, support the mine.

Foreign Trade

Panama buys more from abroad than it sells, a process that creates a trade deficit, or imbalance. In the early twenty-first century, for instance, Panama annually imported about $6.7 billion worth of goods and exported about $5.9 billion.

With no natural oil resources, Panama must import fuel for vehicles. It also imports electronic and transportation equipment. Its most important exports are bananas, sugar, shrimp, coffee, and finished clothing.

Transportation

Panama has about 6,250 miles (10,000 km) of roads, with about 40 percent of them paved. The Transisthmian Highway links Panama City and Colón. The Pan American Highway, which travels north and south through Central and South America, runs through Panama for 339 miles (545 km), from Costa Rica to the town of Chepo. Engineers have not yet extended this road through Darién and into Colombia. The Darién Gap is the last remaining unfinished sector of the highway.

The Panama Canal remains Panama's most famous transportation facility. Large oil tankers and modern freighters, however, are too large for the Panama Canal, which cannot accommodate ships more than 106 feet (32 m) wide. Although a commission has studied the possibility of widening the canal, no plans have yet been drawn up for this project. Because huge oil tankers can't use the canal—and the shipment of oil is important to Panama's economy—in 1982 Panama built an oil pipeline across the isthmus. This pipeline allows tankers to unload their cargo on one side of the isthmus and transfer it to tankers on the other side.

The Chiriquí Railroad, which carries passengers as well as freight, runs in the western half of the country and links Panama with Costa

The **oil pipeline** transports oil across the Isthmus of Panama to a large oil tanker.

Rica. The Panama Railroad—the original line completed in 1855 across the isthmus—carries freight as well. It has also become an important tourist attraction, allowing visitors to follow the route of the Panama Canal across the isthmus.

Panama built its national airport, the Tocumen International Airport, in 1978 on the outskirts of Panama City. This airport serves destinations in Europe, North America, and South America, and also links Panama to the rest of Central America.

ROLLING THROUGH PANAMA

In the late 1990s, Panama privatized (sold to private business) the once-crumbling Panama Railroad. Two U.S. companies bought the railroad, repaired the track, and refurbished the old train cars, adding new passenger cars and an observation car. The new railroad carries passengers in air-conditioned comfort from Panama City to Colón in less than an hour.

The Future

The final transfer of the Panama Canal from the United States to Panama at the end of 1999 marked a turning point in Panamanian history. For the first time, Panama was able to benefit fully from the operation of the canal. The transfer also brought a sense of accomplishment to Panamanians, who saw themselves finally slipping out from the economic and cultural shadow of the United States.

At the start of the twenty-first century, optimism was a common sentiment in Panama. But the country has not seen many of its goals fulfilled. The economy has struggled with slow growth and heavy debts. Political infighting and scandals have eroded Panamanians' confidence in their leaders. Panama's role as an international trade and banking center has made it dependent on the world economy. By the one-hundredth anniversary of Panamanian independence, in 2003, this economy was struggling, with fears of war and terrorism slowing trade across the oceans and through the Panama Canal.

Panama will always be vulnerable to economic and political events outside its borders. For that reason, Panamanians have a sense of uncertainty. But their strong sense of pride and independence will help Panama achieve a peaceful and more prosperous future.

8000 B.C. Indigenous tribes live in present-day Panama.

A.D. 1000 The Kuna Indians move to the San Blas Islands and nearby coastal regions from their former home in northwestern South America.

1501 Spanish explorers Rodrigo de Bastidas, Juan de la Cosa, and Vasco Núñez de Balboa sail along the Caribbean coast of Panama.

1502 Columbus lands in the Darién region.

1510 Spaniards establish colonies along Panama's Caribbean coast.

1513 Balboa crosses the Isthmus of Panama and becomes the first European to see the eastern shores of the Pacific Ocean.

1519 The Spanish governor Pedro Arias de Ávila establishes Panama City on the Pacific coast.

1572 Sir Francis Drake's forces attack Nombre de Dios.

1668 Henry Morgan's forces attack Portobelo.

1671 Henry Morgan's forces sack and burn Panama City.

1699 William Paterson arrives in Darién to establish a Scottish colony.

1799 Alexander von Humboldt arrives in Central America.

1819 Colombia wins its independence from Spain.

1821 Panama declares its independence from Spain and becomes part of Gran Colombia.

1849 A gold rush begins in the United States. Thousands of miners bound for California cross the Isthmus of Panama.

1850 A U.S. company begins construction of the Panama Railroad across the isthmus.

1855 The Panama Railroad is completed.

1882 A French company directed by Ferdinand de Lesseps, the builder of the Suez Canal, begins construction of a canal across the Isthmus of Panama.

1889 Lesseps's company goes bankrupt, and construction of the canal ceases.

1903 The United States and Colombia negotiate a treaty granting the United States the right to build a canal across Panama. The Colombian legislature refuses to approve the treaty. Panama declares its independence from Colombia. The United States signs a canal treaty with Panama.

1906 U.S. construction crews begin creating the Panama Canal.

1914 The Panama Canal is completed.

1925   The Kuna Indians win the right to govern their own
        territory on the San Blas Islands.

1935   The University of Panama is founded in Panama City.

1936   Panama and the United States sign the Hull-Alfara Treaty, changing
        the terms of the canal agreement.

1939   World War II begins in Europe. The United States builds more than one
        hundred military bases in Panama to protect the canal.

1950s   Black Panamanians demonstrate against discrimination in the Canal Zone.
        U.S. administrators deport them from the zone.

1952   The National Orchestra of Panama is founded in Panama City.

1955   The Eisenhower-Remón Treaty again revises the terms of the Panama Canal
        agreement.

1959   Anti-U.S. riots break out in Panama.

1964   Panamanians riot when U.S. schoolchildren refuse to raise Panama's flag in the
        Canal Zone.

1968   Colonel Omar Torrijos Herrera takes power in Panama after overthrowing the
        elected president, Arnulfo Arias Madrid.

1977   The United States and Panama sign two new canal treaties. These treaties call for
        Panama to take control of the Canal Zone in 1979 and the canal in 1999.

1979   Panama takes control of the Canal Zone.

1983   Manuel Noriega becomes head of the Panamanian Defense Forces.

1988   The United States charges Noriega with drug trafficking.

1989   U.S. armed forces invade Panama and capture Noriega.

1999   Mireya Elisa Moscoso Rodríguez becomes Panama's first female president.
        Panama takes over control of the Panama Canal.

2001   Divers discover the *Vizcaina*, one of Christopher Columbus's ships, off
        Panama's Caribbean coast.

2004   Martín Torrijos, son of former dictator Omar Torrijos, is elected president
        of Panama.

COUNTRY NAME Republic of Panama

AREA 29,157 square miles (75,517 sq. km)

MAIN LANDFORMS Atlantic Lowlands, Azuero Peninsula, Barú Volcano, Bocas del Toro Archipelago, Central Highlands, Darién Mountains, Majé Mountains, Pacific Lowlands, San Blas Islands, San Blas Mountains, Tabasará Mountains

HIGHEST POINT Barú Volcano, 11,401 feet (3,475 m) above sea level

LOWEST POINT Sea level

MAJOR RIVERS Balsas, Chagres, Changuinola, Chiriquí, Chucunaque, San Pablo, Sabana, Santa María, Tuira

ANIMALS butterflies, crocodiles, harpy eagles, macaws, monkeys, parrots, quetzals, sloths

CAPITAL CITY Panama City

OTHER MAJOR CITIES Colón, David, Santiago, Chitré

OFFICIAL LANGUAGE Spanish

MONETARY UNITY Balboa. 1 balboa = 100 centesimos. (U.S. paper money and coins are also used.)

CURRENCY

Panama began minting its own currency in 1904 and named its money in honor of the explorer Vasco Núñez de Balboa. By law, one balboa always equals one U.S. dollar. The balboa is divided into 100 centesimos. The government mints coins in 1, 2.5, 5, 10, 25, and 50 centesimos and 1 balboa. It does not print any paper money in balboas. Instead, people use U.S. paper money in Panama. They also use U.S. coins.

Manuel Amador Guerrero, Panama's first president, designed Panama's flag in 1903. His wife, Maria Ossa de Amador, sewed the first flag. The flag is a rectangle divided into quarters. On the top left is a five-pointed blue star, standing for honesty and virtue. On the bottom right is a five-pointed red star, standing for law and order. The top right section is solid red, and the bottom left is solid blue. The colors blue and red stand for the country's first two political parties, while white stands for peace between them. Blue also stands for the waters of the Caribbean Sea and Pacific Ocean, while red stands for the blood of national heroes shed in the cause of independence.

Panama's National Anthem, "Himno Istmeño," or "Hymn of the Isthmus," was written in 1903 by Jerónimo de la Ossa and set to music by Santos Jorge. It became Panama's national anthem in 1925. The anthem is sung in Spanish. Here is an English translation of the first two stanzas and the chorus.

It is necessary to veil with a curtain
The Calvary and Cross of the past,
And for you to adorn the azure of your skies
With the splendid light of concord.

Progress fondly touches your homes,
In time with the music of a sublime song.
You see, roaring at your feet, two oceans
Which give direction to your noble mission.

We finally attained victory
In the happy field of union.
With glowing splendour,
The new nation is illumined.

For a link to a site where you can listen to Panama's national anthem, "Hymn of the Isthmus," go to www.vgsbooks.com.

Flag   National Anthem

Famous People

MANUEL AMADOR GUERRERO (1835–1909) The first president of Panama, Amador led the country from 1904 until 1908. Born in Cartagena, Colombia, he was trained as a doctor. In the summer of 1903, he conspired, with the help of the United States, to free Panama from Colombian rule. As president of Panama, he signed the Hay-Bunau-Varilla Treaty, which set the terms of U.S. ownership and operation of the Panama Canal.

JUSTO ARROYO (b. 1936) Arroyo is a popular novelist born in Colón. His most famous work is *La Gayola (The Jail)*, which appeared in 1966. In *Dedos (Fingers)*, published in 1971, he used a variety of experimental writing techniques, such as using several different narrators, writing in different styles, and changing the flow of time. Arroyo has also published several books of short stories.

RUBÉN BLADES (b. 1948) Blades is an actor, politician, and popular musician who helped introduce Latin American salsa music to the United States. Born in Panama City, Blades began singing with the group Conjunto Latino at the age of eighteen. He earned a law degree from the University of Panama in 1974. After moving to the United States, he recorded *Siembra*, one of the best-selling salsa records of all time. As an actor, Blades starred in his first film, *Crossover Dreams*, in 1985 and has since appeared in *The Two Jakes, Cradle Will Rock*, and more than twenty other movies. He ran for president of Panama in 1994 and took third place.

COQUI CALDERÓN (b. 1937) Calderón is an artist born in Panama City. She attended Rosemont College in Pennsylvania and later studied art and art history in Paris, France. Influenced by European artists of the mid-twentieth century, she developed an abstract style, in which landscapes and human forms blend into solid geometric shapes. After living in Paris, New York, and Miami, Calderón returned to live in Panama in the late 1990s. She has exhibited her works in New York, Miami, and Panama City.

ROD CAREW (b. 1945) Baseball player Carew was a star infielder for the Minnesota Twins and the California Angels. Born in Gatun in the Canal Zone, Carew moved to the United States with his family in 1961. His Major League Baseball career began with the Twins in 1967, when he won American League Rookie of the Year honors. His playing career ended in 1985. He was elected to the National Baseball Hall of Fame in 1991.

ROQUE CORDERO (b. 1917) Panama's leading twentieth-century conductor and composer, Cordero was born in Panama City. He studied conducting in the United States and later became the director and conductor of the National Orchestra of Panama. He won international recognition with his First Symphony in 1947. He has written many works for a full orchestra as well as chamber works for small groups of string and wind instruments.

ROBERTO DURAN (b. 1951) Duran, a boxing champion, was born in Guarare. He took up boxing as a youth and turned professional at the age of sixteen. By 1972 he had won thirty straight victories. In that year, he became the world lightweight champion, a title he held until 1979. Duran went on to become welterweight champion in 1980, junior middleweight champion in 1983, and middleweight champion from 1989 until 1990. In 1990 he lost a famous welterweight title bout against Sugar Ray Leonard, ending the fight by saying "No mas!"—"No more!" Duran retired in 2002 with a record of 104 wins and only 16 losses.

ROBERTO LEWIS (1874–1949) A painter born in Panama City, Lewis studied art in Paris as a young man. He returned to Panama in 1912 to paint murals inside several public buildings, including the National Theater and the Governor's Palace. He was the official portrait painter for the presidents of Panama from 1904 to 1948. He also founded the National Academy of Painting in 1913, serving as its director until 1938.

MIREYA ELISA MOSCOSO RODRÍGUEZ (b. 1946) Moscoso was the first female president of Panama. Born in Panama City, she grew up in Pedasi, the daughter of a schoolteacher. After graduating from high school in the early 1960s, Moscoso began working on the campaigns of President Arnulfo Arias Madrid. She later moved to Miami, Florida, with him and married him. In Florida, Moscoso studied interior design. Widowed in 1988, she returned to the United States and became a leading member of the Arnulfista Party. She won the Panamanian presidency in 1999, vowing to reduce poverty, improve education, create jobs, and run the Panama Canal efficiently.

JOSE BENJAMIN QUINTERO (1924–1999) Stage director Quintero was born in Panama City. He moved to the United States to attend college. Quintero founded the Circle in the Square theater in New York and helped establish New York's off-Broadway theater district for new and experimental plays. He also won fame for directing the plays of American playwright Eugene O'Neill. For his work on and off Broadway, Quintero was nominated for four Tony awards—annual awards presented for distinguished achievements in theater.

AFRO-ANTILLEAN MUSEUM This museum in Panama City honors the Caribbean laborers from Jamaica, Martinique, and Haiti who worked on the Panama Canal. Visitors can see photographs of construction as well as historic crafts and household items.

BALBOA PARK This famous park is in downtown Panama City. Balboa Park is a favorite spot for visitors and city residents, who come to stroll, greet friends, and people watch.

MI PUEBLITO This site on the outskirts of Panama City includes reproductions of typical Panamanian, Caribbean, and Indian villages. The villages include houses, shops, and street scenes. Visitors can learn about the history, arts, and social life of Panama's different ethnic groups.

OLD PANAMA This area contains the ruins of the old Panama City, founded in 1519 and sacked by Henry Morgan in 1671. Visitors can see the remains of a colonial mansion, a cathedral, and a government building.

PANAMA CANAL The canal runs from Colón on the Caribbean coast to Panama City on the Pacific Ocean coast. Visitors can view the canal and ships from several points, including an overlook at the Miraflores Locks on the northeastern edge of Panama City.

PEARL ISLANDS This chain of 90 named and 130 unnamed islands lies southeast of Panama City in the Pacific Ocean. The area is well known for its oysters, which produce some of the finest and largest pearls in the world. Visitors can snorkel and scuba dive in the crystal clear waters surrounding the islands.

PIPELINE ROAD This famous nature trail within Soberiana National Park runs along the eastern banks of the Panama Canal, alongside an old, unused oil pipeline. Every year around Christmas, area birdwatchers hold an annual bird count, sometimes spotting as many as 525 different species.

SAN BLAS ISLANDS This chain of 378 islands stretches along Panama's Caribbean coast, from the Gulf of San Blas to the Colombian border. The islands are home to the Kuna Indians, who have held onto their original language, customs, and clothing and who govern the islands themselves. Visitors can tour the islands by canoe or motorboat and browse for indigenous crafts, including colorful cloth molas.

TABOGA ISLAND Lying 12 miles (20 km) south of Panama City, the island is home to large flocks of brown pelicans and an abundance of flowering trees and shrubs. Hikers can follow several trails through the forests. The island is also a good place for snorkeling, kayaking, and scuba diving. It is nicknamed the Island of Flowers.

artifact: a human-made object that remains from a particular historical period

cacique: an indigenous Central American chief

canal: a human-made waterway

colony: a territory governed by a distant nation and inhabited in part by settlers from that nation

conquistador: a leader of the Spanish conquest of the Americas

coup: a sudden, violent overthrow of a government by a small group

criollo: a Latin American person of pure Spanish descent

deforestation: the process of clearing forests of most or all trees

gross domestic product: the value of the goods and services produced by a country over a period of time, such as a year

hydroelectric power: electricity produced by the power of rushing water. People often dam rivers to create hydroelectric power stations.

indigenous: native to a particular place

isthmus: a narrow strip of land connecting two larger land areas

junta: a small group that rules after a government takeover

literacy: the ability to read and write

lock: a chamber used to raise or lower boats as they move through a canal

mestizo: a Latin American person of mixed Spanish and Native American heritage

oligarchy: a small group of rulers running a nation largely for their own benefit

privateer: a pirate who operates with permission of a government that seeks to harm a rival nation

rain forest: a forest growing in an area of year-round warmth and abundant rainfall

segregation: the official separation of different racial or ethnic groups in places such as schools, restaurants, and hospitals

xenophobia: fear and hatred of strangers or foreigners

Glossary

Selected Bibliography

The American Society of Panama, 2004.
http://www.amsoc.org/ (January 2004)
This website is created for English-speaking people living in Panama. It gives information on family and community events, business issues, educational opportunities, and other topics of interest to U.S. citizens and other English-speakers in Panama.

Barry, Tom. *Panama: A Country Guide.* Albuquerque, NM: Inter-Hemispheric Education Resource Center, 1990.
This book offers general and detailed background information on the geography, history, culture, government, and economic system of Panama. It is written for U.S. diplomats and business travelers.

DuTemple, Lesley A. *The Panama Canal.* Minneapolis: Lerner Publications Company, 2003.
Part of the Great Building Feats series, this book tells the story of the building of the Panama Canal. The author describes the years of planning, frustration, dangers, and hard work that finally resulted in the canal's completion in 1914.

Earle, Peter. *The Sack of Panama: Sir Henry Morgan's Adventures on the Spanish Main.* New York: The Viking Press, 1981.
The author describes Morgan's adventures in the Caribbean and Panama, giving details on the rivalry of England and Spain and the colonial economies of these two empires in the New World.

Greene, Graham. *Getting to Know the General: The Story of an Involvement.* New York: Simon and Schuster, 1984.
The author, an acclaimed British novelist, describes his relationship with Colonel Omar Torrijos, Panama's former leader and strongman.

Knapp, Herbert, and Mary Knapp. *Red, White, and Blue Paradise: The American Canal Zone in Panama.* New York: Harcourt, 1985.
Two American teachers who lived in the Canal Zone during the 1960s describe the area's cultural and social upheavals of that time, when Panamanians began demanding control over the zone and the Panama Canal.

Lindsay-Poland, John. *Emperors in the Jungle: The Hidden History of the U.S. in Panama.* Durham, NC: Duke University Press, 2003.
A history of U.S. involvement in Panama, this book gives details on military and economic intervention going back to the nineteenth century. The author also describes how the United States carried out secret weapons testing in Panama in the late twentieth century.

Lonely Planet World Guide: Panama, 2004.
http://www.lonelyplanet.com/destinations/central_america/panama/ (January 2004)
This site offers information for travelers to Panama, including background information on weather, money, and clothing; holidays and special events; places and sights of interest; environmental issues; and travel both to and within the country.

McCullough, David. *The Path between the Seas: The Creation of the Panama Canal,* **1870–1914. New York: Simon and Schuster, 1978.**
The author describes the earliest surveys of the isthmus by engineers searching for the best route for the canal, the effort by Ferdinand de Lesseps to dig a sea-level canal, and the support of the Panamanian independence movement by the United States.

Noriega, Manuel. *America's Prisoner: The Memoirs of Manuel Noriega.* **New York: Random House, 1997.**
The former leader of Panama, who was captured by the United States and put on trial, gives his own side of the story. Noriega describes how he began his career as a military officer and close ally of the United States, how he ruled Panama in the 1980s, and the events leading up to the 1989 U.S. invasion of Panama that ended with his arrest.

Panama: A Country Study, **2004.**
http://memory.loc.gov/frd/cs/patoc.html (January 2004)
This site offers a useful research guide to Panama, with information on its history, geography, society, environment, culture, economic issues, and politics. The site is produced by the Library of Congress.

Panama News, **2004.**
http://www.thepanamanews.com/pn/v_09/issue_16/frontpage.html (January 2004)
The on-line version of Panama's leading English-language newspaper, this site includes news, opinion, art and concert reviews, sports, classified ads, and a calendar of events.

Panama Sights, **2004.**
http://www.coralys.com/panama/ (January 2004)
This website has a wide variety of general information on Panama, from ancient history to modern everyday life. It offers useful links to companies and media outlets in Panama with websites of their own.

Perez-Venero, Alex. *Before the Five Frontiers: Panama from 1821 to 1903.* **New York: AMS Press, 1978.**
This title provides a history of Panama from Colombia's independence from Spain in 1821 to Panama's independence from Colombia in 1903. The author finds his main theme in the neglect of the region by Colombia's leaders and the frustrated drive for Panamanian independence.

Behnke, Alison, Griselda Aracely Chacon, and Kristina Anderson. *Cooking the Central American Way*. Minneapolis: Lerner Publications Company, 2005.
This book offers easy-to-make recipes from Panama and other Central American countries, along with lots of interesting cultural information about the region.

Bio Explorations
http://www.bioexplorations.com/
This site is operated by a nonprofit organization dedicated to preserving the coral reefs of Costa Rica and Panama. The site includes detailed information about coral reefs and mangrove trees, as well as current information on preservation projects.

Chambers, Veronica. *Marisol and Magdalena: The Sound of Our Sisterhood*. New York: Hyperion Books for Children, 2001.
This book tells the story of a young Latino girl from New York who travels to Panama for a year in a search for her father. The book describes the struggles of living in a family divided between two continents and two cultures.

DuTemple, Lesley A. *The Panama Canal*. Minneapolis: Lerner Publications Company, 2003.
This book gives a detailed history of the building of the Panama Canal.

El Canal de Panama/The Panama Canal
http://www.pancanal.com/
This website is dedicated to the Panama Canal, with information on the canal's history and current engineering projects, news releases, a photo gallery, radar weather images, and webcams offering views of the canal twenty-four hours a day.

Farman, John. *The Short and Bloody History of Pirates*. Minneapolis: Lerner Publications Company, 2003.

This book covers the history of pirates with comic cartoon illustrations and humorous anecdotes and facts.

Griffin, Adele. *Rainy Season*. New York: Hyperion Books, 1998.
This story tells of a young girl living on a U.S. Army base in the Canal Zone. She witnesses the violence and conflict between Panamanians and "Zonies"—United States citizens living and working in the Canal Zone but not affiliated with the U.S. Army—as the canal is passed to the government of Panama.

Haynes, Tricia. *Panama*. New York: Chelsea House, 1998.
This book for young researchers give background facts on the history, climate, population, and cultural life of Panama.

Marrin, Terry. *Terror of the Spanish Main: Sir Henry Morgan and His Buccaneers*. New York: Penguin Putnam Books for Young Readers, 1999.
This is a well-researched portrait of the Englishman Henry Morgan and his adventures as a pirate, thief, and all-around scoundrel in the Spanish colonies of the seventeenth century.

Further Reading and Websites

McNeese, Tim. *The Panama Canal.* **San Diego: Lucent Books, 1997.**
This book looks at the canal's construction, the struggle for Panamanian independence, and the issues raised by U.S. control of the canal in the twentieth century. The text is illustrated by historical photographs, several sidebars, and a useful timeline.

Panama Tours
http://www.panamatours.com/
This site offers a virtual tour of Panama, covering the Panama Canal, rain forests, beaches and coastal areas, folklore and culture, indigenous villages and reservations, and the biggest shopping mall in Central America.

Panama Women and Children in Need
http://www.pwcin.com/
Panama Women and Children in Need is a nonprofit agency that assists poor children and families in Panama. Its Web page briefly describes education, health, and antipoverty programs taking place in Panama.

Primate Foundation of Panama
http://www.primatesofpanama.org/
This foundation carries out research, education, and conservation programs on the country's primate species. The website includes full-text articles, a census of primates in Panama, and information on the Primate Rescue Center, which shelters abandoned pet primates.

Rau, Dana Meachen. *Panama.* **New York: Scholastic, 1999.**
This book provides an overview of Panama's culture, government, and history for young readers.

Rink, Paul. *The Land Divided, the World United.* **New York: Julian Messner, 1963.**
This book offers an illustrated account of the building of the Panama Canal.

vgsbooks.com
http://www.vgsbooks.com
Visit vgsbooks.com, the homepage of the Visual Geography Series®. You can get linked to all sorts of useful on-line information, including geographical, historical, demographic, cultural, and economic websites. The vgsbooks.com site is a great resource for late-breaking news and statistics and is regularly updated.

Welsbacher, Anne. *Life in a Rain Forest.* **Minneapolis: Lerner Publications Company, 2003.**
This book describes the ecosystems of rain forests, how human activities have affected these forests, and what is being done to protect them.

Winkelman, Barbara Gaines: *The Panama Canal.* **New York: Scholastic Library Publishing, 1999.**
Winkelman offers a description of the building of the Panama Canal, the economic consequences of its operation in the twentieth century, and the struggle between the United States and Panama over who should own and operate the canal.

Captions for photos appearing on cover and chapter openers:

Cover: These cottages on the coast of Panama have thatched roofs that are common to homes throughout rural areas of the country.

pp. 4–5 Panama has 1,700 miles (2, 745 km) of coastline. Tourists come to the area for many forms of recreation including fishing, boating, and snorkeling.

pp. 8–9 Mountains dominate the landscape of central Panama. These mountains are viewed from the Pan American Highway, which runs from Alaska to the southern tip of South America.

pp. 20–21 Ruins of a cathedral stand in Old Panama City, which was destroyed by English pirate Henry Morgan in 1671. The city was rebuilt a few miles from this original location.

pp. 38–39 Schoolchildren wearing uniforms gather in a school yard on the San Blas Islands.

pp. 46–47 A procession in Panama City celebrates the Feast of Corpus Christi.

pp. 58–59 The Panama Canal is a major source of income for Panama. Here the *Vistafjord* cruise ship goes through the Pedro Miguel Locks on the Pacific Ocean end of the canal.

Photo Acknowledgments

The images in this book are used with permission of: © Art Directors/Les Hannah, pp. 4–5; Ron Bell/Digital Cartographics, pp. 6, 11; © Victor Englebert, pp. 8–9, 13, 14, 20–21, 44, 46–47, 50 (top), 53, 54, 62 (bottom), 68; © Carrol Henderson, pp. 10, 15, 17, 42–43; © Joshua Sjogren, pp. 12, 48–49, 55; Library of Congress, p. 22 (LC-USZ62-51767); Institute of Jamaica, p. 24; © Independent Picture Service, pp. 28–29, 30; Laura Westlund, p. 27; © CONTIFOTO/CORBIS, SYGMA, p. 32; Jimmy Carter Library, p. 34; © Bill Gentile/CORBIS, p. 35; © Reuters/CORBIS, p. 36; © Maxine Cass, pp. 38–39, 50–51 (bottom); © Art Directors/A Tjagny-Rjadno, p. 40; © Carlos Reyes-Manzo/Andes Press Agency, pp. 41, 51 (top), 60, 62 (top), 64; © Art Directors/Robert Belbin, pp. 58–59.

Front cover image: © Richard Hamilton Smith/CORBIS; Back cover image: NASA.